Cambodia and the International Community

Cambodia and the International Community

The Quest for Peace, Development, and Democracy

Edited by
Frederick Z. Brown and
David G. Timberman

INSTITUTE OF SOUTHEAST ASIAN STUDIES, Singapore

Copyright ©1998 by Asia Society.

Published in the United States by Asia Society
725 Park Avenue
New York, NY 10021-5088
E-mail: angelac@asiasociety.org
World Wide Web: http://www.asiasociety.org

Published in the Republic of Singapore by
Institute of Southeast Asian Studies
30 Heng Mui Keng Terrace, Pasir Panjang
Singapore 119614
E-mail: publish@iseas.edu.sg
World Wide Web: http://www.iseas.edu.sg/pub.html
(for exclusive distribution in Southeast Asia, Japan, Australia, and New Zealand)

Library of Congress Cataloging-in-Publication Data

Cambodia and the international community/edited by Frederick Z. Brown and David G. Timberman.

1. Cambodia—Politics and government—1975—. 2. Cambodia—Economic conditions. 3. Cambodia—Economic policy. 4. Nongovernmental organizations—Cambodia.
I. Brown, Frederick Z.
II. Timberman, David G.
DS554.8 C176   1998   sls98-26208

ISBN 0-87848-532-5 (Asia Society, USA)
ISBN 981-230-030-9 (ISEAS, Singapore)

Contents

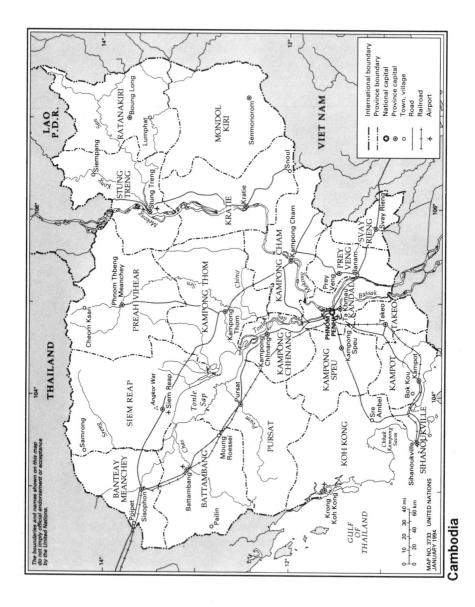

Cambodia

Preface

Cambodia has a place in many peoples' consciousness to a degree far in excess of what might be expected given the country's small size and limited economic and strategic importance. The reasons for this are not difficult to identify. First, many people continue to be haunted by the tragedy of the genocide committed in Cambodia *by Cambodians.* The worldwide attention paid to the "trial" and recent death of Pol Pot, the brutal leader of the murderous Khmer Rouge, underscored not just the extent of the world's awareness of the atrocities committed in Cambodia, but also their relative recentness. Second, in stark contrast to the recent tragedy of Cambodia, there is its historical glory reflected in the breathtaking temples at Angkor Wat, as well as in the proud traditions of its people. And third is Cambodia's experience as a victim at the hands of more powerful international forces. Cambodia has been repeatedly forced to capitulate to larger and more powerful nations and to forces beyond its control—including misguided ideology and shifting great power relations. Sadly, it is the combination of these conflicting factors that gives Cambodia lasting resonance.

Aware of Cambodia's recent tragic past and concerned for the country's uncertain future, in early 1996 the Asia Society, Johns Hopkins' Paul H. Nitze School of Advanced International Studies (SAIS), and the Asia Foundation initiated a project on Cambodia and the International Community: The Road Ahead. In keeping with the Society's tripartite goal of informing policymakers, educating the American public, and encouraging dialogue among Asians and Americans, the project consisted of a major international conference held in Washington, D.C. in March 1997, public programs in New York, Long Beach, California, and Washington, D.C., and publication of this volume. While the release of *Cambodia and the International Community* concludes this particular project, during 1998 the Asia Society and SAIS are continuing to address developments in Cambodia and in U.S. policy toward Cambodia through a series of occasional meetings and short reports.

The project on Cambodia and the International Community has been a highly rewarding collaborative venture. The project would not have got off the ground without the initial collaboration between the Asia Society and SAIS. It has been the Society's pleasure to work with two longtime friends at SAIS, Karl Jackson and Frederick Brown. The success of the international conference was in large measure due to the participation of the Asia Foundation, which funded the travel of many of the Cambodian participants and provided invaluable substantive and logistical advice. The Society greatly appreciates the enthusiastic involvement of Asia Foundation staff Jon Summers in Phnom Penh and Nancy Yuan and Rudi Jeung in Washington.

The project was also fortunate to receive other generous and timely financial support. An initial grant from the United States Institute of Peace allowed us to undertake the overall project. The Center for International Political Economy funded a portion of the conference costs. Finally, a grant from the Patrick Gerschel Foundation funded a portion of the international conference and the public programs. Each of these contributions was critical to the success of the project; the absence of any one of them would have significantly reduced the scope and quality of project activities.

A number of individuals played key roles in the development and administration of this project. David Timberman, consultant to the Asia Society, conceived of the project and managed its varied components, from fundraising to coediting this volume. Fred Brown, the other codirector and coeditor, graciously lent his vast experience and expertise to all aspects of the project. Its sometimes complicated administration was always capably handled by Lois Weiss at SAIS, Sam Borin at the Asia Foundation office in Phnom Penh, and Andrew Thornley at the Asia Society.

The contents of this volume reflect the high level of commitment and care shown by all the contributors. A number of small but significant factual gaps were filled by last minute research assistance from Alisa DiCaprio and Sophie Richardson. And finally at the Asia Society, Karen Fein, Editor for Policy and Business Programs, and Rayne Madison, Designer, are to be credited with turning an unruly manuscript into a published volume in record time. As Cambodia approaches these important elections, we hope that the book will provide worthwhile background information and shed useful light on the road ahead for this beleaguered nation.

Kevin F. F. Quigley
Vice President for Policy and Business Programs
Asia Society
June 1998

Introduction: Peace, Development, and Democracy in Cambodia— Shattered Hopes

Frederick Z. Brown and David G. Timberman

When this collection of essays was conceived in mid-1996 our purpose was to assess the progress made by Cambodians and the international community to bring peace, development, and democracy to Cambodia. At that time there was some sense of accomplishment but also growing concern about the future. Unfortunately 1997 was a dismaying year for most Cambodians and those in the international community who care about Cambodia. By spring 1997, when the first drafts of many of these essays had been written, it had become apparent that the intensification of political conflict in Cambodia was rapidly undermining the gains of the previous four years. The March 30 grenade attack on a peaceful opposition rally signaled both a qualitative escalation of political violence and, in hindsight, the jettisoning of peaceful political methods to determine who would lead Cambodia into the twenty-first century.

By 1997 it also had become clear that the commitment and coherence of the international community interested in Cambodia had begun to wane. Many of the countries initially involved no longer had common interests in Cambodia's internal affairs. The reasons are not hard to identify. First, after 1993, Cambodia was no longer the critical crossroads of the cold war and it threatened neither regional stability nor great power relations. Second, donor fatigue set in. The international community had handed the Cambodian parties a way out of their painful mess—it was now up to them to reconcile, to reorder their society, and to work their way up the development ladder the way the rest of Southeast Asia had. The tepid response of the international community to the March 30 attack reflected its growing weariness and did little to discourage the further use of force.

The July 1997 coup effectively ended the awkward power-sharing arrangement that had existed since 1993 and dealt a severe blow to Cambodia's nascent democracy. The abrupt removal of First Prime Minister Norodom Ranariddh by Second Prime Minister Hun Sen meant that the reins of power were once more in the grasp of a Leninist party with little concern for either human rights or the fledgling sense of participatory governance that had been implanted, however tentatively, through the UN process four years before. To the Cambodian people—racked by decades of war and civil strife, still impoverished, and already deeply uncertain—the destruction of the coalition government brokered by the UN-sponsored peace process, with peremptory abductions and sudden executions, was a revisitation of the horrors of the 1970s.

Much of what had been accomplished by the international community's multiyear, multibillion-dollar investment in Cambodia consequently has been destroyed. And with Hun Sen expected to win the elections scheduled for July 1998, Cambodians and the international community, and of course the contributors to this volume, have been forced to confront the prospect of a Cambodia once again under the control of an authoritarian leader and a government staffed at the policy level by former members of the Khmer Rouge or the Communist Party between 1979 and 1991.

In response to what happened in July 1997, we felt it imperative to ask our contributors to recast and expand their essays to address more painful and urgent questions: What went wrong? What might have been done differently? What constructive role, if any, can the international community play in Cambodia, given the sad state of affairs in that country? While answers to these questions are in a sense speculative, we believe certain conclusions are warranted. This introduction provides an overview of Cambodia's recent political history to give nonspecialists the context for the essays that follow. It introduces some of the book's major themes and offers some reflections on the lessons that might be drawn from the Cambodian experiment in making and maintaining peace and what role the international community realistically might be expected to play in the future.

The Persistence of the Past

The roots of the Cambodia tragedy are to be found in the geography of Southeast Asia; in the centuries of national and ethnic rivalry among Khmers, Thais, and Vietnamese; and above all in a culture of zero-sum absolutism that refuses to admit the possibility of a "loyal opposition" in political life. One can glimpse the tragic predicament of Cambodia in 1998 reflected in the history of the Khmer Empire beginning in the ninth century as well as in the authoritarian habits of a civilization that flourished almost a millennium ago.

In David Chandler's essay, the persistence of Cambodia's past is applied to the Cambodia of today. The carved stone galleries of Angkor Wat bear witness to the historical struggle of the Khmer Empire to preserve its preeminence in continental Southeast Asia. First conquering, then fighting off the incursions of the Siamese, the Cham, and later the Vietnamese, the Khmer Empire collapsed in the early fifteenth century and was picked apart by its neighbors until it became a French protectorate in 1864. When Cambodia gained its independence from France in 1955 Prince Norodom Sihanouk guided his kingdom through the perils of the cold war in Indochina and sustained minimum damage compared with the disasters that befell Vietnam and Laos.

In 1970 Sihanouk was deposed. Cambodia entered a downward spiral that led to the autogenocide of the Khmer Rouge (1975–78) and to the Vietnamese invasion and occupation (1978–89). With the installation of a pro-Vietnamese government in Phnom Penh in January 1979, a new era in Indochina began. For noncommunist Southeast Asia, particularly the Association of Southeast Asian Nations (ASEAN), the creation of a Marxist-Leninist regime responsive to Vietnamese political will and the influence of the Soviet Union (still a major force in regional geopolitics in the early 1980s) was unacceptable.

With the explicit support of China and the United States ASEAN encouraged two Cambodian factions exiled in eastern Thailand: the Khmer People's National Liberation Front (KPNLF) and the Unified National Front for an Independent, Neutral, Peaceful, and Cooperative Cambodia (FUNCINPEC). The KPNLF was republican in spirit; FUNCINPEC was monarchist. In 1979 they were joined by the remnants of the Democratic Kampuchea government, the Khmer Rouge, still steadfast in their radical

Maoist-communist ideology and implacably hostile to the Vietnamese. From their safehavens in Thailand, the three groups organized small armies that conducted guerrilla insurgencies against the Vietnamese and the People's Republic of Kampuchea in Phnom Penh. The Khmer Rouge soon came to dominate the political entity created by ASEAN in 1982, the Coalition Government of Democratic Kampuchea (CGDK), which enjoyed support from ASEAN, China, and the United States. Vietnam, backed by the Soviet Union and the East European Bloc, supported the Phnom Penh regime. The Cambodia struggle had become simultaneously a civil war, a regional war, and a great-power proxy war.

Between the two opposing communist factions—the exiled Khmer Rouge and the ruling Phnom Penh regime, backed by Vietnam—there was mortal enmity. Because of the outcome of the war in 1975, which had either forced them to flee or to suffer the depredations of the Khmer Rouge, the noncommunists hated both their Khmer Rouge coalition colleagues and the Phnom Penh regime, staffed largely by ex–Khmer Rouge. It is safe to surmise that most Cambodians felt deep hostility toward one or more of these principal actors responsible for their plight. Yet given the society's Buddhist culture, which stresses the spirit of forgiveness, the Cambodian peasantry comprising the great bulk of the population was no doubt more prepared to make peace than were its political leaders. But before 1991, the fundamental obduracy and hunger for unshared power on the part of the elite leadership of all the Khmer parties concerned made compromise and national reconciliation impossible. It is this same recalcitrance that occasioned the July 1997 coup and has made a lasting political settlement extremely difficult in contemporary Cambodia.

The Paris Accords and UNTAC

The collapse of the Soviet Union and end of the cold war precipitated a negotiated end to the war in Cambodia. The East European Bloc had been the main supporter of Vietnam's military capability and economic development as well as the life-support system of the Phnom Penh regime itself. As Soviet influence in Southeast Asia eroded, the Chinese found it expedient to modify their geopolitical priorities and downgrade the primacy of the Cambodia issue. In September 1989 the Vietnamese army withdrew from Cambodia, satisfying the demands of ASEAN, China, and the United States. China, still smarting from the international outcry over Tiananmen Square, sought to normalize relations with several Southeast Asian states, the Soviet Union, and Vietnam. Vietnam, nearly bankrupt and rife with mounting domestic discontent, was desperately promoting normalization with its ASEAN neighbors, China, and the United States.

The sea change in global and regional relations made it both desirable and possible for the United States, China, ASEAN, and Vietnam to enter into negotiations to remove Cambodia as a bone of contention. The result was the Accords on a Comprehensive Political Settlement of the Cambodia Conflict, signed in Paris on October 23, 1991, and their subsequent application under the United Nations Transitional Administration in Cambodia (UNTAC). The Paris Accords called for UN-administered elections to form a new government in Cambodia, ordained that the Cambodian political system be organized on the basis of liberal democratic principles, and committed the international community to assist with the reconstruction and development of Cambodia's shattered economy.

The Khmer parties to the Paris Accords were swept along on the tide of the determination of the external powers—for their own reasons—to remove the Cambodia conflict from center stage. External events associated with the winding down of the cold war preoccupied the main players in the Cambodian peace process as momentum toward a political settlement mounted. The architects of the Accords turned a blind eye to Cambodia's most intractable internal aspects, deciding that these could not be resolved at a UN conference table but rather through a process of genuine reconciliation among the Khmer parties themselves. Pragmatically the Accords may have been the most feasible compromise under the international political conditions prevailing in 1991—but they left the fundamentals unchanged, and UNTAC was charged with the task of enforcing an extraordinarily complex, time-phased scenario predicated on an environment of conciliation and compromise among the Khmer parties that did not, in fact, exist. No tradition of compromise had ever existed between mortal enemies in Cambodia's political culture. From the outset this reality made genuine national reconciliation a distant goal.

In addition, the five permanent members of the United Nations Security Council (PermFive) failed to give the Accords the teeth necessary to guarantee compliance. For example, to ensure a neutral political environment UNTAC was ordered to exercise direct supervision over all "existing administrative structures" acting in the fields of information, foreign affairs, national defense, and public security. Clearly this was the most difficult civil mandate to execute, yet it was the one the framers of the Paris Accords were most negligent in addressing, leaving it instead to the judgment of UNTAC's high command. Whatever powers the secretary-general's special representative, Yasushi Akashi, possessed were in practice circumscribed by the PermFive who had bartered the precarious peace arrangement. Many in the UN felt that by pushing the incumbent Phnom Penh regime too vigorously on a neutral political environment, the chances for peace might be ruptured. And the Khmer Rouge, which had signed the Paris Accords in October 1991 but opted out in early 1992, remained a force that, if challenged too bluntly, could bring down the effort. All it would take, so the conventional wisdom went, was a few Khmer Rouge attacks against the 19,000-man UN military force and the deliberate targeting of international civilian peacekeepers.

If the great powers no longer deemed the game worthwhile, the underlying issues certainly were not forgotten by the Cambodians. The political environment during the election campaign period of 1993 was far from neutral. The phased cantonment and disarmament of the Khmer factions' military forces stipulated by the Paris Accords had not been accomplished, nor had the key ministries of the existing State of Cambodia government been subject to effective UNTAC supervision. The Cambodian People's Party (CPP) militias and political operatives were in a position to exert pressure, indeed outright coercion, on the population and against their principal rivals, FUNCINPEC and the Buddhist Liberal Democratic Party (BLDP, the renamed KPNLF). Scores of Cambodians were killed and hundreds were injured by political violence during the UNTAC period, some by the Khmer Rouge but most as a result of CPP actions.

The extraordinary care with which the machinery of the electoral process was put in place by UNTAC's electoral component and, indeed, the actual feat of carrying off the national elections successfully masked the harsh antagonisms embedded in Cambodian society. Technically the elections were the most meticulously planned, most expensive per capita ever held in Asia. UNTAC's voter registration achieved a 95 percent (of those deemed eligible) rate of participation nationwide. In the election held May 23–29, 89.4 percent of registered voters cast their ballots. With a total of 38.2 percent of the vote and 51 seats in the Constituent (later the National) Assembly, the CPP came in second to FUNCINPEC's 45.5 percent and 58 seats. The results were a shock to the incumbent CPP, which had expected to win, and an astounding display of courage on the part of the Cambodian people.

UNTAC chief Akashi rejected the CPP's charges of fraud and, on June 10, 1993, declared that the elections were fair and free. The CPP refused to accept defeat. A secession attempt in early June by eight eastern provinces had to be quashed by the UN. It was evident to many in the international community that the incumbent CPP regime still controlled the bulk of military force, the police, and civilian administration; that the CPP was determined not to surrender power; and that FUNCINPEC—the winner of the election—controlled too few guns and administrative and political cadres to assume power countrywide. In the absence of a large additional investment of UN military forces and the virtual takeover of the Cambodian government by UNTAC, some sort of accommodation to these circumstances would have to be made. Without it Cambodia would revert to civil war and social chaos—a real possibility in June 1993.

Power Sharing

The implicit quid pro quo of the Paris Accords in 1991 (in effect to gain Soviet and Vietnamese cooperation) had been that the incumbent CPP would have a fair shot at political dominance if it would go along with the rules of the game of UNTAC and abide by the results of the election. Hun Sen and the CPP had expected to win in May 1993, and indeed UNTAC officials and the international community generally had similar expectations. Hun Sen did not win, and he was obliged to become second prime minister to FUNCINPEC's Ranariddh. The convoluted power-sharing arrangement, which in effect led to the creation of dual governments, shaped the course of Cambodian politics from then on.

In summer 1993 FUNCINPEC and the CPP joined in a provisional interim government, and the newly elected constituent assembly wrote a new constitution. This process, along with the divvying up of ministerial posts and governorships, became a test of the uneasy reconciliation. Both parties in effect were forced to make a coalition government work, if only to avoid renewed conflict and obtain the several billion dollars of international financial assistance that had been promised to rebuild the country as part of the understandings reached at Paris. David Ashley's essay, and those of David Chandler and Michael Doyle as well, describe the tribulations of the coalition government between Ranariddh's FUNCINPEC and Hun Sen's CPP that emerged in 1993.

After the new Royal Government of Cambodia (RGC) was formed in October 1993, the UN and the international community remained directly engaged in the reconstruction and development of Cambodia. The country's development needs were great—per capita GNP was only $220 in 1993—but given Cambodia's limited absorptive capacity they were well within the bounds of international donor capability. The International Committee on the Reconstruction of Cambodia (ICORC), the consortium of international donors, had pledged $880 million in economic assistance at its founding meeting in June 1992. Most official bilateral and multilateral aid was directed to budget support, training, education, infrastructure repair, and basic social services. Kao Kim Hourn's essay catalogues the benefits and costs of this massive international intervention.

Increased international assistance made it possible to begin to rebuild Cambodia's shattered physical and human infrastructure; economic reform and Cambodia's reconnection to the regional economy fueled respectable economic growth. Naranhkiri Tith's essay reviews the improvements in Cambodia's macroeconomic performance but cautions that Cambodia's economic recovery is threatened by a lack of political accountability and transparency, the absence of a fair and competent judicial system, and a bloated and underpaid bureaucracy. Judy Ledgerwood discusses the challenges of socioeconomic development in rural areas, where 85 percent of all Cambodians live.

Only a few international donors continued to actively support the development of democracy in Cambodia. The UN Center for

Human Rights (UNCHR) became a key defender of human rights, and a flock of nongovernmental organizations, many of them American, supported programs promoting human and women's rights, judicial reform, legislative development, media professionalism, and civil society. As Lao Mong Hay observes in his essay, for a brief period it appeared that democracy might take root in Cambodia. But the emphasis of most donors was squarely on Cambodia's economic development, the theory being that the prospect of an improved economy (if not prosperity) would eventually promote political harmony—a familiar theme for postconflict societies. The international community's interest in the political situation diminished as the months passed. With sovereignty fully vested in the new coalition government, the external signatories to the Paris Accords were not inclined to exert overt pressure with regard to the human rights abuses that became increasingly apparent. There was a sense that it was up to the Cambodians themselves to effect true reconciliation.

In 1994 and 1995, however, the possibility of making donor aid conditional was raised in ICORC's private councils in response to continuing human rights issues, rampant corruption on the part of both coalition partners, illegal logging, and the misdirection of revenues to the Ministry of Defense. The International Monetary Fund (IMF) and the World Bank eventually took action on illegal logging but with unsatisfactory results. The rape of Cambodia's forest resources, which is described in detail in Kirk Talbott's essay, continues in 1998 with devastating consequences: A recent report by Global Witness, a British environmental NGO active in Cambodia, estimates that forest hardwood reserves will be completely exhausted shortly after the turn of the century.

From Coalition to Coup

By 1996 it was all too evident that the pluralist political system and representative government codified in the 1993 constitution had not become part of the Cambodian political system as had been planned, perhaps naively, by the framers of the Paris Accords. The National Assembly had been considered the fundament of a nascent civil society. In 1996 it had become virtually powerless in the face of the CPP's dual tactic of intimidation and financial co-option of Assembly members, Ranariddh's deplorably inept leadership, and the venality and gross corruption of both the CPP and FUNCIN-PEC.

While the CPP cadres often were factionalized, they nonetheless managed, in true Leninist style, to keep disagreement in-house to present a relatively united front to their political foes. FUNCIN-PEC, on the other hand, was openly splintered by criticism of Ranariddh and weakened by the firing of Minister of Finance and Economy Sam Rainsy, which in turn led to defections and eventually to Rainsy's formation of the Khmer Nation Party (KNP). In October 1995 FUNCINPEC's general secretary (and the government's foreign minister), Prince Norodom Sirivudh, was accused of a plot to assassinate Hun Sen. He was jailed, then driven into exile. Soon thereafter Rainsy was expelled from the National Assembly. Hun Sen pursued a cunning divide-and-conquer strategy, pulling off defections of FUNCINPEC and BLDP figures, such as Khieu Kanarith and Ieng Mouley. Consequently the CPP increasingly dominated the coalition with FUNCINPEC and the BLDP, its minor partner.

Signals pointing to a national meltdown became explicit when the leadership of the Khmer Rouge (still with military forces at their command and base areas in the north and west) began to fragment. By the summer of 1996 almost half the Khmer Rouge military force broke from Pol Pot and defected to the government. The following year the faction's leadership broke into bitter dispute, eventually causing Ta Mok, the guerrilla commander, to arrest Pol Pot. David Ashley points out that the resulting competition between FUNC-INPEC and the CPP for the allegiance of defecting Khmer Rouge leaders and the units they commanded was significant to the deterioration of cooperation between the coalition partners, and it eventually became the final rupture in the personal relationship between Ranariddh and Hun Sen.

On March 30, 1997, a peaceful KNP rally in front of the National Assembly was subdued by forces using hand grenades. Nineteen persons were killed, a hundred wounded, and Sam Rainsy barely escaped with his life. From this point onward any semblance of cooperation between the coalition partners ceased. Even the most optimistic analysts saw little chance for political reconciliation and assumed that, sooner rather than later, violence would again shape the future of the country.

On July 5, 1997, the CPP initiated a series of events that either killed or drove into exile many of the political leaders and senior provincial cadres of FUNCINPEC, the BLDP, and the KNP. Hun Sen's special CPP units sought out and arrested or summarily executed key members of the opposition (the UNCHR reported 41 people were killed with many dozens more unaccounted for). First Prime Minister Ranariddh and about twenty FUNCINPEC, BLDP, and KNP politicians and members of the National Assembly managed to flee to Thailand. The July coup came as no surprise to most Cambodians or foreign observers who had been following the nation's affairs since the 1993 elections. Hun Sen's compulsion for power was no secret. But the timing and tactics of the coup were uncertain, and the brutality and totality with which it was carried out were stunning.

The reaction of the international community was surprisingly strong. ASEAN, which has the most direct interest in Cambodia, postponed Cambodia's membership in the regional grouping, making it the only Southeast Asian nation to be excluded. ASEAN has had an interest in bringing an end to the conflict in Cambodia, which has extended to border disruptions and the flight of refugees. Moreover ASEAN has not wished to see a government in Phnom Penh that caters to the international illegal narcotics trade and grand scale money laundering. Reflecting these concerns, ASEAN formed an ad hoc "troika," composed of the foreign ministers of Thailand, Indonesia, and the Philippines, to launch a diplomatic initiative intended to persuade Hun Sen to reconcile with Ranariddh and to hold free and fair elections. In spirit this initiative broke precedent with the long-standing ASEAN principle of noninterference in a member country's affairs, although Cambodia technically was not a member.

With strong U.S. urging, international financial institutions suspended loans to Cambodia, and, in what was possibly the greatest blow to Hun Sen, the UN decided to leave Cambodia's seat vacant at the opening of the General Assembly in October. Several Western donors withdrew their bilateral assistance to the Cambodian government, although some have continued aid to the nongovernmental sector. The crisis also prompted the creation of the "Friends of Cambodia," an informal diplomatic group whose members had been key players in the Paris Accords, including the United

States, Australia, Canada, China, the European Union (EU), Japan, and Russia. Both ASEAN, through the troika, and the Friends of Cambodia stressed to Hun Sen the importance of creating and maintaining a neutral political environment for free, fair, and credible elections. Japan took an uncharacteristically active role by brokering a deal that satisfied Hun Sen's demand that Ranariddh be tried for his alleged crimes (it was done in absentia) and still allowed Ranariddh to return to Cambodia to contest the elections (by virtue of a pardon by King Sihanouk).

The 1998 Elections

As this volume goes to press, elections are scheduled for late July 1998. Once again, as they were in 1993, Cambodians and the international community are looking to elections to resolve an internal conflict and to legitimize the country's leadership through the ballot box. This task, which fell tragically short of its aim the first time, is all the more difficult now because the 1998 elections are the first that Cambodia has attempted to conduct on its own. Little is left of the UNTAC electoral infrastructure, and the involvement of the international community will be severely diminished in comparison to that of 1993.

Moreover the willingness and ability of the Hun Sen government to conduct genuinely free and fair elections is in doubt. The CPP dominates the bureaucracy and the security forces and has effectively censored the media. While opposition parties, NGOs, and journalists are, in theory, free to challenge the government, they do so at their own peril. A National Election Commission (NEC) has been created, but the opposition perceives it to be strongly weighted toward Hun Sen—despite the membership of a prominent human rights activist. Beyond the issue of political coloration, there are widespread doubts that the commission can handle the logistical challenge of managing elections in so little time. In addition the opposition is itself disorganized and factionalized. Although it would be difficult for any political group to overcome the obstacles presented by the CPP machinery, it will be even more difficult if the opposition doesn't come together. Opposition leaders, primarily Ranariddh and Rainsy, publicly hold out the possibility of boycotting the polls.

The UN and the EU have agreed in principle to assist the government in conducting the elections but reserve the right to reverse their decision if conditions warrant. That UN Secretary-General Kofi Anan has taken a strong stand with regard to international observation of the 1998 elections indicates that the UN sees the UNTAC experience as a significant precedent for peacekeeping—if the UN is seen to fail in Cambodia, can it be expected to succeed elsewhere? The U.S. government, skeptical of Hun Sen's commitment to free and fair elections, has directed its assistance to Cambodian NGOs planning to monitor the elections. As this volume goes to press, no central authority, such as the UN, has assumed responsibility for certifying whether the elections are free and fair. However, certification—or even an informal assessment of an election's outcome—requires a network of election observers to produce credible data as well as agreement on the standards for determining if an election is free. In the upcoming elections, it appears there will be neither a massive international monitoring effort nor an international consensus on criteria for judging the returns. In the event that Hun Sen wins in an uncompetitive or boycotted contest, the United States, Japan, ASEAN, the EU, and other key international actors will need to decide if they will accept the outcome and establish normal relations with the new Hun Sen government. The probability that the United States, Japan, and ASEAN will adopt differing approaches to this issue suggests that the relative cohesion exhibited by the international community since the July 1997 coup is unlikely to survive the July 1998 elections.

Lessons from the Past

Why, after such an immense effort on the part of the UN and the international community at large, did Cambodia spiral down from 1993 to the tragic denouement of July 1997? One reason, surely, is the relative shallowness of the accomplishments of the UN during the period of its authority on the ground in Cambodia. The UN might, with some justification, respond that never had so much money and effort been expended for so few people for so long in order to heal a war-ravaged society. But several chapters of this book offer a litany of specific reasons for UNTAC's partial failure, for example: slow deployment of UNTAC, the difficulties in executing the progressive phasing of the UNTAC process, the failure to disarm the parties, the bickering over bringing economic assistance to

Cambodia during the UNTAC period, the weakness of the UNTAC civil police component, and the difficulties in monitoring and countering human rights abuses by the CPP. As David Ashley points out, by 1991 the Cambodia conflict "was a dispute left over from the cold war, not a reaction to it." It was not as much an ideological conflict as a struggle for power between feudal lords funded and supplied by foreign patrons. UNTAC's presence did not change that reality.

More fundamentally the seeds of Cambodia's continuing crisis are found in the Paris Accords themselves, in the international political climate surrounding what was supposed to be the resolution of the Cambodia issue, and in the basic assumptions underpinning what was essentially an exercise in nation building. Three of these assumptions are discussed below.

One assumption was an unrealistic faith in the electoral process as the key to solving the problems of Cambodia's conflicted society. The Paris Accords were premised on a belief that an electoral process under impartial international supervision would act as a legitimizing mechanism for the political arrangement to follow. All political groups would have a chance at power sharing. (The "comprehensive" nature of the Accords, of course, unraveled when, in early 1992, the Khmer Rouge, renounced their participation.) All other aspects of the Paris Accords and UNTAC were subordinate to the central objective of creating a legitimized government through an electoral process. It was assumed, somewhat blithely, that international bilateral and multilateral assistance and NGOs supporting constructive social change would follow this "legitimation" and thereby promote reconciliation between the CPP and the noncommunist parties that had been their competitors, at least to the point where they would not seek to resolve their differences by force of arms.

Unfortunately this was not to be. The political rivalry was too great, and the stakes were too high. Without the Cambodian political elite's genuine acceptance of the need for coexistence, the 1993 elections were in effect a continuation of mortal political conflict by other means. Moreover there was no connection between the elections and the reality of governing Cambodia. Although FUNCINPEC won the election, it could not govern due to the CPP's entrenchment and its own organizational weaknesses. Thus, a

FUNCINPEC victory had the unintended effect of virtually ensuring the continuation of instability rather than bringing about an environment of political compromise that would lead eventually to economic progress and social calm. Finally, the international community retreated from its commitment to establishing a genuinely legitimate government when it acquiesced to Hun Sen's demands for power sharing.

The 1993 elections also failed to inculcate new democratic norms and behavior among the Cambodian political leadership. By allowing King Sihanouk and Hun Sen to, in effect, set aside the electoral outcome, the international community became a party to an act that sent a clear message that power politics, not the rule of law, would continue to prevail in Cambodia. UNTAC, then, offers an obvious but important lesson for future UN peacekeeping efforts elsewhere: Elections are necessary for democracy but by no means sufficient. Without broad, sustained supporting measures over a long period, elections by themselves cannot promote liberal democracy in a historically conflicted society.

A second questionable premise was that power sharing would work in Cambodia's highly conflictual and zero-sum political environment. The collapse of Cambodia's coalition government raises basic questions about the utility of power sharing— as least as practiced in Cambodia—as a way to build peace and democracy in highly conflictual societies. (In retrospect it was premature to view Cambodia as a "postconflict" society between 1993 and 1997.) The FUNCINPEC-CPP government was not a coalition in the normal sense. The leaders of the two parties were bitter rivals. In effect two national governments were established, while the CPP continued to dominate the army, the internal security machinery, the national bureaucracy, and local government. The creation of these dual governments bloated the bureaucracy, fueled corruption, and politicized even further the military and security forces. This phony political accommodation crippled decision making and created an environment inimical to effective governance. In sum power sharing in Cambodia did not foster reconciliation; it did not promote trust or build confidence; and it did not create a new, more inclusive political center.

The failure of power sharing speaks to the difficulty of operationalizing political institutions and processes based on the rule of law, political pluralism, and nonviolent political competition in situations where the political elite evinces little or no commitment to these values. In retrospect it is clear that the coalition government created in September 1993 should have been subjected to the same international scrutiny as the election that was so meticulously carried out under UNTAC.

A third mistaken assumption made by most international donors following the elections was that an emphasis on economic development—rather than on further political development—would ensure peace and stability in Cambodia. High-level international support for the democratization of Cambodian government and society declined precipitously following the elections. Having expended immense effort, generally applauded as successful, the UN moved on to other urgent peacekeeping challenges (in Bosnia and central Africa). The focus of most international donors shifted to Cambodia's reconstruction and economic development not its continued political development. Moreover the international community's assistance to Cambodia's reconstruction and development was largely disconnected from the performance of its government and leaders. This approach has been proven to be erroneous.

The international community, perhaps under stronger leadership from the ICORC, should have made a significant portion of multilateral aid contingent upon bureaucratic reform, reduction of the army, cessation of timber cutting, and so forth. And greater emphasis should have been placed on building up countervailing centers of legitimate authority (for example, the Constitutional Council, which is mandated by the 1993 constitution) and by paying more attention to helping the National Assembly become an effective branch of government.

Challenges for the Future

To return to the basic themes of this volume, what will it take to bring peace, development, and democracy to Cambodia? The uncertainties surrounding the elections scheduled for July make it both difficult and unwise to speculate about Cambodia's short- to medium-term future. It can be said, however, that noncompetitive or violent elections that result in an oppressive one-party government will not advance the prospects for peace and development in Cambodia. Regrettably this scenario or some variation of it appears to be likely. With this prospect Cambodia and the members of the international community concerned with Cambodia face five challenges, the handling of which will play a major role in determining the prospects for peace, development, and democracy.

Perhaps the most immediate challenge will be to protect and, if possible, deepen Cambodia's nascent civil society. Many fear for the future of Cambodian NGOs dedicated to promoting human rights, democratization, and the rule of law. Press freedom is also in jeopardy. The international community has funded, trained, and encouraged thousands of Cambodians to believe that these values have a place in their country and should be respected. Many Cambodians have promoted these values at considerable risk to themselves and their families. They deserve the continued support and protection of the international community.

The need to protect Cambodia's civil society is just the most urgent aspect of a larger and more difficult challenge: reforming Cambodia's autocratic and intolerant political culture. Cambodia's political elite must come to understand that both the nation's and their own fortunes are better served over the long run by pluralistic and nonviolent political competition. Cambodia's history of colonialism, monarchy, radicalism, and communism makes this a difficult concept for many in its ruling circles. It may be that this will be possible only with the passage of time, leadership, and generational change. But the international community can support the process of political change by helping to ensure the vitality and efficacy of political institutions designed to channel competition and strengthen the rule of law, such as the National Assembly and the newly established Constitutional Council.

The third challenge facing Cambodia and the international community is restarting the nation's economy and putting in place economic policies conducive to sustainable economic development. Cambodia remains one of the world's poorest and least developed countries. It still suffers from the serious damage done to its human resources by the Khmer Rouge. Since mid-1997 its economy has been further hurt by the triple blows of political uncertainty, the suspension of foreign aid and World Bank/IMF loans, and the regional financial crisis.

There is cause for both concern and hope regarding the Cambodian economy. The reasons for concern are multiple. First, the commitment of the Hun Sen government to transparent and market-driven economic policies is open to question. Second, bureaucratic inefficiency and corruption will continue to be encumber on entrepreneurship. Third, foreign investment and economic aid are likely to be in short supply, especially if political conflict and high-level corruption persist. All of this may cause Cambodia's economy to become even more dominated by illegal logging and the narcotics trade. Arrayed against this disturbing prospect are two reasons for hope. First Cambodia is situated in the center of a region that, while presently facing economic setbacks, is likely to return to moderate growth within a year or two. Second, between 1994 and 1996, there was significant improvement in the economy and economic policymaking. At least this gives the country an economic foundation upon which to build.

The fourth challenge is the handling of the remnants of the Khmer Rouge, particularly the treatment of those responsible for the genocide of the 1970s. The backbone of the Khmer Rouge has been broken, and they no longer pose a major threat to security. However, the Khmer Rouge can affect the short-term political situation in Cambodia in two ways. First, their lingering presence gives the government a rationale for maintaining a counterinsurgency campaign and a continued role for the armed forces in domestic security. And since the factions were not demilitarized during the peace process earlier in the decade, the possibility remains of using the armed forces against political enemies other than the Khmer Rouge. Second, reintegrating the members of the Khmer Rouge into Cambodian society will continue to be a complex and controversial issue. The reintegration of mid- and lower-level Khmer Rouge guerrillas should be encouraged and supported. But the reintegration of the Khmer Rouge leadership, particularly those responsible for the genocide and starvation of the 1970s, is fraught with moral and political problems. The sad reality is that the reintegration of these Khmer Rouge leaders may be accepted by Cambodia's conflict-weary society. But the failure of the Cambodian government to conduct a meaningful accountability exercise will almost certainly further undermine whatever belief in justice Cambodians continue to have as well as reduce the government's international respectability.

The final challenge is the need to address the highly politicized nature of the state apparatus, in particular the armed forces. The greatest shortcoming of the UNTAC period was the failure to demobilize the factions and depoliticize the Royal Cambodian Armed Forces. Two actively partisan armies were left intact, barely coexisting under the thin veneer of a national military. This helped to set Cambodia up for the events of last July. It is highly unlikely that this situation can be addressed, much less remedied, as long as political tensions in Cambodia remain high. However, when there is political will to downsize and depoliticize the bureaucracy and military, the international community should offer its support to the fullest extent.

The essays that follow address these and other issues in greater detail and offer a variety of perspectives on the continuing struggle to bring peace, development, and democracy to Cambodia.

The Burden of Cambodia's Past

David P. Chandler

Introduction

For a historian writing of Cambodia in early 1998 there is little reason for optimism about the country's future. A pessimistic—even alarmist—stance seems justified by recent political events as well as by the persistence of problems, such as Cambodia's runaway birth rate, declining natural resources, short-sighted environmental policies, and failure to enact and enforce effective civil and criminal codes. In addition the last thirty years have been bleak, and for Cambodians the weight of the recent past in particular has been difficult to bear.

Almost twenty years after the end of the Khmer Rouge era (1975–79), Cambodia's society and people continue to suffer from the physical and psychological traumas of that period. In less than four years, over 1.5 million Cambodians died from malnutrition, overwork, misdiagnosed diseases, and executions. The real number will never be known and could easily be higher. The regime's anti-urban, anti-"bourgeois" purges decimated Cambodia's small elite and destroyed the fragile trust that existed among different segments of the population. Its dogmatic, vengeful policies and ham-fisted administration hastened the deaths of hundreds of thousands of men, women, and children. Tens of thousands of others were executed as "class enemies" or "spies." When the regime was driven from power, fear of the Vietnamese, weariness, socialism, and the promise of safety drove half a million survivors to seek asylum overseas. Cambodia's institutions, not robust in the best of times, were smashed or abandoned and had to be rebuilt from scratch.

Progress in the 1980s was extraordinary, considering the magnitude of what had happened and the scarcity of resources available to the new, Vietnamese-sponsored regime, isolated by the quarantine imposed on it by allied nations hostile to Vietnam. At the same time, the new government treated its opponents harshly, and for several years Cambodia was closely monitored by Vietnamese officials.[1] In the meantime, tens of thousands of Khmer Rouge soldiers, refugees, and dependents were encamped along both sides of the Thai-Cambodian border. They posed a baleful threat to Cambodia, inflicted thousands of casualties on Vietnamese and Cambodian forces sent to oppose them, and were a source of unfocused but severe anxiety for millions of Khmer. The discredited Khmer Rouge and their unrepentant leaders flourished for a decade under the patronage of China, Thailand, and the United States. Calls from smaller nations to bring Pol Pot and his colleagues to justice for their crimes against humanity were repeatedly brushed aside in the interests of realpolitik. Recent calls for a trial of the Khmer Rouge leadership emanating from some of the people who stonewalled the idea for many years may ring a little hollow.

Since the 1970s hundreds of thousands of land mines, strewn across the landscape by the Khmer Rouge and their opponents, have been another source of trauma. The mines have maimed and killed thousands of people. They also have made thousands of hectares of land uncultivable, roads hazardous, and marketing goods a perilous undertaking. The mines continue to cripple and kill dozens of Cambodians every month. Twenty years of internecine warfare have left Cambodia with one of the world's highest numbers of widows as heads of families. The psychic damage of these wars and of the Khmer Rouge era on survivors, certainly of mammoth proportions, can never be assessed.

Cambodia continues to stagger under the weight of a range of fundamental problems that are rooted in the nation's location and history. These problems—which collectively constitute the heavy burden of Cambodia's past—include its physical vulnerability, the deceptive lure of its history, and its volatile political culture, which suffers from a bizarre blend of tyranny and dependence. This chapter will address the sources and major implications of these problems.

Cambodia's Historic Vulnerability

At least two of the obstacles to peace and progress in Cambodia— its physical vulnerability and its location between Thailand and Vietnam—are insuperable givens that have affected the country for several hundred years. Cambodia's borders have always made it vulnerable to invasion and accessible to immigrants. Its limited resources—timber, fish, gemstones, and so on—can be exploited relatively easily and quickly. Cambodia's geographic vulnerability, along with the small size of its population, heightens its people's sense of insecurity vis-à-vis their neighbors and restricts Cambodian governments to a cautious, evenhanded foreign policy.

Since the 1780s, if not earlier, Cambodia has been harassed, dominated, protected, exploited, and undermined by Thai or Vietnamese regimes. The involvement of these two countries in Cambodia's affairs intensified in the early nineteenth century as the newly installed dynasties in Bangkok and Hue grew strong, competitive, and ambitious. In the 1830s and 1840s the wars fought between them on Cambodian soil devastated the smaller kingdom and weakened its fragile institutions. Had the French not imposed their protection in 1863, Cambodia might have disappeared as an independent state, with its territory divided into Thai and Vietnamese zones of influence, perhaps by the Mekong.[2]

With French intervention, Thai influence diminished. Vietnamese involvement persisted in another guise. France quarantined Cambodia from Siam and tied the country's export economy to that of southern Vietnam, which the French called Cochin China. Ethnic Vietnamese had greater access than Cambodians to French-language education and occupied favored positions in the protectorate's civil service. "Indochina," made up of three segments of Vietnam plus Laos and Cambodia, was a French concoction dominated by its Vietnamese components. The idea that Vietnam, with independence, might inherit a Vietnamese-controlled federation was pleasing to many Vietnamese nationalists and to the Indochina Communist Party (ICP) founded by Ho Chi Minh in 1930.

For a decade or so, the ICP pursued a purely Vietnamese agenda. Until armed struggle against the French broke out in 1946, very little was done to activate party branches in Laos or Cambodia. As the struggle gathered momentum, the ICP's leaders started to think in Indochinese terms, and Laos and Cambodia became battlefields. Indigenous communist parties were founded by the Vietnamese in both countries in 1951. Statutes for them were drafted in Vietnamese. At the time most Lao and Cambodian cadres were already fluent in the language. Cambodian communists, like the Lao, were told that their struggle was part of a wider international revolution and they would benefit from ongoing Vietnamese guidance. Many young Cambodian recruits enjoyed being empowered in this way.[3]

Cambodian nationalists, on the other hand, were suspicious of Vietnamese intentions and sometimes fanned anti-Vietnamese feelings among fellow Khmer. In altered form the tension between such racially fueled rhetoric and the internationalist, protective agenda that Vietnam fostered among Cambodian radicals engendered the factionalism of the coalition government that existed until July 1997.

Relations with Thailand in the colonial era were insignificant, especially after 1907 when France made Thailand relinquish the provinces of Battambang and Siem Reap, which Cambodia had ceded in the 1790s. In 1941, after France's defeat in Europe, the Thai reoccupied most of the lost territory. They were forced to give it up again five years later; but when Cambodia became independent in 1954 Thailand was reluctant to accept that its satellite of the 1840s was now a sovereign state.

In the Norodom Sihanouk era (1941–1970) the Thai government supported several plots for his overthrow. One was led by Sam Rainsy's quixotic father, Sam Sary. Thai support for General Lon Nol, who deposed Sihanouk in 1970, was halfhearted, despite his anti-communist credentials. As good students of realpolitik, the Thai maintained polite relations with the Khmer Rouge. When the Vietnamese invaded Cambodia in 1979, Pol Pot and several thousand Khmer Rouge troops found refuge on Thai soil. The Thai government, by then allied with China, welcomed the newcomers, hoping to please China and destabilize the Vietnamese protectorate in Phnom Penh. Under Sino-Thai patronage, uncontested by the United States, the Khmer Rouge rebuilt its army, attracted international support (e.g., from the United Nations), and waged war against the Vietnamese. In the 1990s the Thai–Khmer Rouge alliance enabled Thai entrepreneurs to exploit Cambodian gem and timber resources worth hundreds of millions of dollars.

With this unsavory, instrumentalist record, it seems likely that Thailand's policies toward Cambodia in the future will have a more harmful impact than any that might be developed by Hanoi. Vietnam's once grandiose political interests in Cambodia seem to have faded along with any dreams the Vietnamese may have had of a socialist grouping of Indochinese states. "Indochina" is dead. Vietnam, like Cambodia, now seems more interested in becoming a good citizen of Southeast Asia, sharing the benefits that may accrue from joining ASEAN. At the same time Vietnamese exploitation of forests in eastern Cambodia and immigration into the country will probably maintain present levels or increase. In the process, ethnic tensions are bound to erupt, intensified by demographic pressures and fanned by irresponsible politicians.

Historical relations between Cambodia and its neighbors will not determine Cambodia's future, but there are aftereffects. Many Cambodians believe that Vietnam poses a greater threat to Cambodia than Thailand and suggest that while Thai exploitation is a case of "what you see is what you get" the Vietnamese agenda is deeper and more devious. Evidence for such beliefs is hard to locate but the suspicions remain in force. "The Vietnamese are most dangerous," a Cambodian recently told a friend of mine, "when they are invisible."

Military threats to Cambodian sovereignty have diminished but Cambodia will never be militarily strong enough or populous enough to withstand pressures from Vietnamese immigrants and foreign entrepreneurs. In the process, its resources will be wantonly depleted. From an environmental point of view, the prospects for Cambodia's medium term future are bleak.

The Misleading Lure of the Past

The lure of the past in Cambodia, a second reason for caution, has often misled many Cambodian leaders, and affects political culture in Cambodia today. The problem stems from colonial times. Beginning in the 1870's, French savants "discovered," mapped and dated hundreds of medieval Cambodian temples and deciphered hundreds of medieval inscriptions written in Sanskrit and Khmer. In the process they constructed a sumptuous, half–forgotten history. Cambodians were informed that their ancestors had built "Angkor" (as indeed they had) and that at one time Cambodia had dominated a large part of mainland Southeast Asia. In the same breath they were told that because of Cambodia's subsequent "decline," they were incapable of governing themselves.

The French claimed that the Khmer lacked the "vigor" of the Vietnamese. Like the Lao, they were seen as "children" who needed ongoing protection; what the Vietnamese "needed" is less clear. In Cambodia, the volatile mixture of bestowed grandeur and bestowed incompetence gave Cambodian nationalism a peculiar, edgy character. Many monks, intellectuals and political figures who found it easier to see themselves as the heirs of Angkor (and thus superior to the supposedly "vigorous" Vietnamese) than as inhabitants of a small Southeast Asian colony that needed to live within its means and to remain at peace with nearby powers.

Sihanouk, Lon Nol, and Pol Pot were prisoners of these illusions. Convinced of Cambodia's incomparability, they assumed that its native grandeur (enhanced by foreign help) could deliver it from the "evil" of Vietnam. All three men embarked on reckless foreign policies that drew on their *folie de grandeur.* Sihanouk, the most realistic of the three, tried to outwit the Vietnamese; Lon Nol and Pol Pot sought to defeat them in battle. All their scenarios were applauded by obsequious hangers-on and foreign patrons for whom Cambodia played a small but helpful part in the global confrontation in which its foreign patrons were wholeheartedly engaged.

Dependence on Foreign Patrons

Another reason for pessimism about Cambodia's future is the perennial dependence of its leaders, until very recently, on foreign powers. Some of the protection imposed by Thailand, Vietnam, and France between the 1790s and 1953 was sought by Cambodia's kings; some of it was thrust upon them. When Cambodia emerged from its colonial cocoon, its leaders, emboldened by what they thought was independence, embarked on a series of relationships with less responsive patrons.

The process of patron seeking began under Sihanouk in 1955, after he abdicated and became a private citizen. Fearful of his neighbors, unsympathetic to the United States, flattered by foreign statesmen, and egged on by his advisers, the prince chose the Soviet bloc and China as Cambodia's new patrons while prudently retaining friendly ties with France and accepting aid from the United States.[4] Helped by these faraway powers he hoped to outwit so-called U.S. imperialism, meet Cambodia's financial obligations, finesse the Vietnam War, and remove the menace of socialism at home.

The game worked for ten years or so, but it was dangerous to play. It contained elements of tragedy, too, for Sihanouk seems to have been aware, as Lon Nol and Pol Pot were not, that patrons make the rules. In all three cases, as throughout Cambodia's history, no patron was willing to jeopardize national interests on Cambodia's behalf. In 1970, despite Lon Nol's expressions of neutrality, Cambodia was flung head first into the Vietnam War. From then on Sihanouk's patrons dropped away. China plotted to set up a Maoist regime in his place; the Soviet bloc offered him nothing; and France merely proposed political asylum. The Vietnamese communists, supposedly his allies in 1970, soon reneged on the agreements they had made with the prince to honor Cambodia's borders. The behavior of patrons in duress should have been a warning to Lon Nol and later to Pol Pot.

It is worth asking in hindsight, however, what else the beleaguered ruler could have done. An alliance with his anti–communist neighbors in the 1960s would have brought Cambodia into the Vietnam War almost at once. A full-blown alliance with the United States would have had the same effect, and one with North Vietnam probably would have provoked a South Vietnamese invasion.

Sihanouk's "neutral" policies, which stemmed from patriotism, vanity, wishful thinking, and wariness, were not as far-fetched or as mercurial as many cold warriors depicted them at the time. The Thais gave the prince no reason to trust them; neither did the warring governments of Vietnam. The United States was unwilling to berate or discourage the anti–Sihanouk policies of its anti–communist allies. Frightened of genuine independence when he was militarily so weak, Sihanouk established networks of dependence through which Cambodia hoped to gain some freedom to maneuver. He compromised his country's sovereignty but did not surrender it. He undermined his neutrality but avoided bloodshed for a while. By 1968, if not sooner, he had run out of room to maneuver.

Dependence also had compromised those who resisted the Sihanouk regime. Those who took a conservative, nationalist perspective, like Sam Sary, Dap Chhuon, and Son Ngoc Thanh, were soon entangled in demeaning alliances with Cambodia's neighbors. Those who hoped to install a socialist regime and eventually did so were held in check by Sihanouk's police and by their indifferent patrons in Hanoi.

When the hapless Lon Nol, came to power in 1970, he was even more dependent. He had an almost mystical faith in the man he called his "personal friend," Richard Nixon, who had written him a few cautiously worded letters of support. Lon Nol believed that Nixon personally could remove the threat of the Vietnamese who he saw as non-Buddhist "unbelievers" and thereby save the Cambodian "race." He also counted on open-ended U.S. military support. In the process he failed to notice that his so-called personal friends were disengaging from the region, never to return, even as they promised their heartfelt, continuing assistance.[5]

Dependency on China dogged the Khmer Rouge leaders after they seized power in April 1975 and sought to escape the party's long-standing subordination to Vietnam. The interplay between communism and nationalism as well as their relation to foreign patronage are such enduring features of Cambodian politics, even today, that the background is worth examining.

In 1954, after the Geneva Peace Conference several thousand resistance fighters and ICP members were evacuated to North Vietnam, pending what their patrons told them would be the collapse of the pro–Western regimes throughout Indochina. Most of the evacuees remained in North Vietnam until 1970. Some stayed even longer. During this time they were nominally led by a veteran Cambodian revolutionary, Son Ngoc Minh, but were not encouraged to develop national policies. Many took Vietnamese revolutionary names, married Vietnamese women, and were seconded to the Vietnamese army.

During the First Indochina War (1946-1954), Vietnamese patronage seemed natural and rewarding to most of these Khmer revolutionaries, and those who took up residence in North Vietnam did so willingly enough. The ones who stayed behind to carry out the political struggle, led by Tou Samouth, were not particularly antagonistic toward Hanoi. For a time, they were optimistic about seizing power. In 1954–55 the collapse of the pro-Western regimes that had just been established in Indochina seemed a distinct possibility to these experienced fighters. The collapse was delayed by U.S. intervention in Laos and Vietnam and by Sihanouk's dexterity, popular appeal, and security apparatus in Cambodia. By 1956 radicals in Cambodia were on the defensive, cut off from their patrons in Hanoi and harassed by Sihanouk's police.

It was at this point that the movement received an infusion of new members returning from university study in France. Several of these men and women—including Saloth Sar (alias Pol Pot), Ieng Sary, and Son Sen—had been drawn toward communism and joined the French Communist Party. When they came home, most of them took up careers in teaching or the civil service and joined the clandestine communist movement. As well-educated, patriotic revolutionaries, they were unwilling to await developments in Indochina or to take guidance from abroad. Political struggle as enjoined by Hanoi offered these ambitious men and women the unpalatable alternatives of inactivity, compromise with Sihanouk's "feudal" regime, or arrest. At the same time, because they lacked weapons, armed struggle was out of the question.[6]

When Tou Samouth died under mysterious circumstances in 1962, Saloth Sar became the leader of Cambodia's small, underground Communist Party. Soon afterward he went into hiding with a handful of colleagues, including Son Sen and Ieng Sary, in "Office 100," a Vietnamese communist military base that shifted back and forth across the Vietnamese-Cambodian border. In the camp, where he lingered for nearly two years, Saloth Sar and several other Khmer Rouge luminaries first encountered hands–on Vietnamese patronage and protection.

Summoned to Hanoi for consultations in mid-1965, Saloth Sar was told when he got there—after a four-month trek up the Ho Chi Minh Trail—that his party's agenda was irrelevant, amateurish, and chauvinistic. The Vietnamese document reporting the event noted that Saloth Sar "said nothing" in reply. After lingering for several months in Hanoi, Sar proceeded to Beijing where he was warmly welcomed by party spokesmen who were about to embark on the Cultural Revolution. His appreciative new patrons told him that his notions of independent revolution were more authentic than the wait-and-see policies suggested by Vietnam.

Back in Cambodia Sar secretly maneuvered his followers into a Maoist political position. He was careful to keep his fences mended with Hanoi, knowing that when the time came to embark on armed struggle, his party would need Vietnam's assistance. The opportunity came in 1970 when Sihanouk fell from power. Vietnamese help was crucial in arming the Cambodian communists, training their forces, and destroying Lon Nol's army, but at the end of 1972 the Vietnamese withdrew their troops as part of their peace agreement with the United States.

Sar and his colleagues, who refused to join the cease–fire, felt abandoned and betrayed. By this time, if not before, they shared Lon Nol's racist antipathy toward Vietnam. Instead of attacking Vietnam directly, however, they secretly purged over a thousand "Hanoi Khmer" who had come from Vietnam in 1970 to help them.

The cease-fire meant, in the words of CIA Director William Colby, that Cambodia was now "the only game in town." For the first nine months of 1973 the country was subjected to intense U.S. aerial bombardment. The bombing had the intended effect of digging a trench around the capital and thus postponed a Khmer Rouge victory. (It took the Khmer Rouge two more years to win the war.) But it also inflicted thousands of civilian casualties, intensified the fervor of Khmer Rouge soldiers, and some have argued, hastened the ascent of Sar's faction within the Cambodian Communist Party. Only the last of these effects is subject to debate.[7] After dropping half a million tons of bombs in a campaign where American lives were not endangered, the U.S. Congress called it off.

In spite of choosing "independence" and "self-mastery" as their mottoes, the Khmer Rouge, when they came to power, could not stand on their own feet—especially after 1977, when Sar, now going by the name Pol Pot, chose to wage war against Vietnam. Once the Khmer Rouge attacks had been launched, the regime needed open-ended Chinese assistance to survive. As previous Cambodian rulers had discovered to their detriment, however, the patronage turned out to be limited and contingent. Pol Pot's regime collapsed when his patrons in Beijing found that the risks of supporting him militarily had become too high. Luckily for the Khmer Rouge, however, China's patronage continued after 1979, with Beijing letting go of its clients only in 1990, in the run-up to the Paris Peace Accords.

In early 1979, in the wake of Vietnam's invasion, Hanoi established a protectorate over Cambodia that shared many characteristics with the French protectorate, including a somewhat altered "civilizing mission" whereby the deserving but "childlike" Cambodians were trained to honor and respect the Vietnamese. Once again, however, foreign patronage proved costly for the patrons, and in 1989 the Vietnamese withdrew. After a transitional period (1990–92) in which Hun Sen rose to power, the Paris Peace Accords ended the era of foreign patronage for Cambodia, but a final flurry of protection—a sort of encore after two centuries of dependency—occurred in 1992–93 under the United Nations Transitional Authority in Cambodia (UNTAC).

In 1993, in the aftermath of the UNTAC-brokered elections, the newly established Cambodian government found itself without a political patron for the first time in centuries, although substantial aid from a range of donors continued to pour into the country. In the mid-1990s the economic dependence of Cambodia's political elites on selected foreign powers, including Thailand, Taiwan, and Malaysia, seems to have replaced political dependence, but the national and political aspects of patronage have become less important. From an ecological and economic point of view, however, the exploitation of Cambodia by outsiders shows no signs of letting up.

Political Culture

Cambodia's political future also might be impaired by its enduring political culture. For hundreds of years absolute rulers have confronted factional opponents, and factions have confronted one another, scrambling to serve their own interests in a volatile, high-stakes game. A winner-takes-all political culture based on endemic distrust has impeded the development of a civil society, stifled free expression, encouraged cronyism and violence, and exacerbated people's tendency to distrust and fear those in power. Seen in this light, Cambodia's strong man, Hun Sen, despite his modern trappings, remains very much a traditional political leader.

In classical Cambodia power was thought of as a finite, expendable commodity.[8] The verb "to govern" was the same as the verb "to consume." There were no legal constraints on the conduct of those at the top. Similarly there was no recourse other than flight or rebellion for people who were exploited. The Cambodian legal code, such as it was, was designed to protect the rich and powerful, particularly the king, against crimes of lèse-majesté.

Under the protectorate, the French froze Cambodia's institutions, including the potentially absolute monarchy, in place and did little to develop the rule of law. When Sihanouk took power in 1955, he paid little attention to laws that impeded his power and rode roughshod over Cambodia's constitution. Political prisoners, held without trial, were frequently executed. None of Sihanouk's successors (nor any of their opponents, for that matter) have felt that they owed much to the electorate or that power was something to be shared or balanced in the interests of the country. Instead Lon Nol, Pol Pot, Hun Sen, and Prince Ranariddh have tended to identify the welfare of the nation with themselves and have seen dissent as tantamount to treason.

Over the years most Cambodian politicians and officeholders have focused their attention on neutralizing their enemies. In modern times none has gone so far along these lines as the Khmer Rouge. Following a Maoist model Pol Pot and his colleagues allowed political warfare to direct Cambodian life. The colossal costs of this fiery experiment are still being measured. One of its very few benefits was to make Cambodians aware that politics was something that impinged on their daily lives and demanded participation. Most Khmer had traditionally associated politics with rich people, corruption, and exploitation; they had not had a voice in political decisions or any power over the nation's political life. The depredations of the Khmer Rouge, for one thing, made it easier for people in the 1990s to conceptualize tyranny, lawlessness, and human rights.[9]

Very few Cambodian leaders (Sihanouk in his heyday was an exception) have thought it necessary to be popular, flexible, or responsive. By and large, injustice and government have gone hand in hand. The people's loyalty is supposed to be unquestioning; power is its own reward. No ruler allowed himself to be doubted. Very few have listened to advice, and none before Pol Pot questioned the distribution of power among haves and have-nots. Pol Pot's response to these imbalances was to kill the haves and empower the have-nots while divesting everyone of possessions. That he felt himself uniquely endowed to do so placed him firmly within Cambodian political culture.

The inequities and corruption in Cambodian society under Sihanouk and Lon Nol, combined with the buffeting Cambodia took from the cold war, were enough to draw thousands of Cambodians—especially intellectuals and young, poor peasants— into the ranks of the communist movement, which, when it took power, swiftly became the least responsive, most unaccountable, and least transparent regime in Cambodia's history.

Similarly widespread resentment against government abuses in the early 1990s, rather than the vague and nostalgic programs offered by the opposition, led millions of voters in 1993 to vote against an armed, incumbent regime for the first time in Cambodian history. Ironically the election produced a form of government (i.e., a coalition), which, while ineffective in many instances and inimical to Cambodia's political culture, postponed the outbreak of civil war, made the losing party somewhat more responsive to people's material needs than it had been, and for a time provided a facade of stability sufficient to placate most donor nations. Since the July 1997 coup these positive aspects of coalition government have all but disappeared, and the two most prominent factions have embarked on a confrontation aimed to eliminate the other. Cambodian history seems intent on perpetually repeating itself as a tragicomic farce.

There seems to be a contrast in many Cambodians' minds between politics as practiced and an imagined form of government based on pure-mindedness, detachment, and justice. In precolonial times, the savior was someone thought to be endowed with merit and magical powers. More recently the ideal government leader has usually been construed as someone personable, detached, and incorruptible. In the 1960s Khieu Samphan's reputation for incorruptibility and responsiveness was a major contributor to his sub-rosa popularity among students, intellectuals, and some of the rural poor. During the same period Pol Pot was admired by his students and colleagues—and, if defectors can be believed, was still admired in the 1990s—for his smoothness, patriotism, and kindly manner, which contrasted sharply to the relentless egotism of Cambodians then in power.

Conclusion: Future Prospects

Hun Sen's July 1997 coup d'état averted the possibility of civil war but also may have foreclosed the possibilities for pluralism in Cambodian political life. Given the power equation in Cambodia today, there seems little likelihood of increased harmony and compromise on the part of those in power or increased freedom of expression and association for ordinary people. The prospects for a genuinely free and fair election in 1998 are as dim as the prospect that the current regime will feel it necessary to reform to gain the voters' trust. In fact, as the country drifts toward elections, and as it loses the favored position it enjoyed with many donor nations, it seems likely that violent incidents like the March 1997 grenade attack will occur whenever anyone in power, especially Hun Sen, feels threatened. Outbursts of violence against the Vietnamese minority cannot be ruled out, although this is less likely than in the recent past. Finally while it is also possible that the armed forces of the former coalition partners will engage in a full-scale conflict—using surrogates enrolled from the ranks of defecting Khmer Rouge—scattered confrontations are more likely than a full-scale civil war.

Are there any countervailing forces in sight? It is possible that modernization, which is impacting so unevenly on Cambodia today, will provide moderating effects through increased access to information, education, and income for larger segments of the population. There are also signs of restiveness, courage, and resiliency among journalists, workers, and nongovernmental organizations pressing for change in, among others, the fields of human rights, industrial relations, and the rights of women. So far the government's response to these pressures has lurched between violence and indifference, but in spite or because of this nongovernmental organizations, their allies, and the causes they work for are increasingly gaining respect.

Perhaps changes will come about as a result of pressure, discreetly applied, from donor nations, although it is impossible to predict what form this pressure might take, the conditions under which it might be applied, or how Hun Sen and Prince Ranariddh might respond.

There are also grounds for some optimism about Cambodia's future, but not much, in what appears to be the disappearance of the Khmer Rouge as a political or military threat. As this is written, the effects of the Khmer Rouge implosion are impossible to predict, but the disappearance of Pol Pot from the nation's psyche may be that baleful figure's first act of kindness to the Cambodian people.

In the short term, however, it is difficult to see how the men and (much more rarely) women who have profited enormously from Cambodia's violent and autocratic political culture so far, and who cling so tenaciously to power, would be willing to see the culture altered. Still such alterations are urgent from the point of view of delivering equity to the Cambodian people, who are, as so often in the past, poorly governed but stubbornly refuse to be "consumed."

Notes

1. See Eva Mysliwiec, *Punishing the Poor: The International Isolation of Kampuchea* (Oxford: Oxfam, 1988), and Michael Vickery, *Kampuchea:*

Politics, Economics and Society (London: Frances Pinter, 1986). Hun Sen, Cambodia's second prime minister, gained power in this period. He is fluent in Vietnamese.

2. For a discussion of this period, see David Chandler, *A History of Cambodia,* 2d ed. (Boulder, CO: Westview Press, 1996), pp. 118–32.

3. Author's interviews in Phnom Penh (January–February 1997) with five Cambodians who joined the ICP and spent the period 1954–70 in North Vietnam.

4. For discussions of Cambodia in this period, see Roger Smith, *Cambodia's Foreign Policy* (Ithaca, NY: Cornell University, 1965), and David Chandler, *The Tragedy of Cambodian History* (New Haven: Yale University, 1991).

5. For a perceptive political history of the Lon Nol period, see Justin Corfield, *Khmers Stand Up!* (Clayton, Australia: Monash University, 1995). The best discussion of U.S. policy in that era remains William Shawcross's *Sideshow: Kissinger, Nixon and the Destruction of Cambodia* (New York: Simon and Schuster, 1979).

6. For a persuasive study of Vietnamese-Cambodian relations between 1946 and 1975, and documentary support for this part of the essay, see Thomas Englebert and Christopher Goscha, *Falling Out of Touch* (Clayton, Australia: Monash University, 1994). See also Ben Kiernan, *How Pol Pot Came to Power* (London: Verso, 1985).

7. See William Shawcross, *Sideshow,* and Ben Kiernan, *The Pol Pot Regime* (New Haven: Yale University, 1996).

8. For an interesting discussion, see Benedict Anderson, "The Idea of Power in Javanese Culture," in *Language and Power* (Ithaca, NY: Cornell University, 1990), pp. 17–77.

9. For a discussion of political culture in the UNTAC era, see Steve Heder and Judy Ledgerwood, eds., *Propaganda, Politics, and Violence in Cambodia* (Armonk, NY: M.E. Sharpe, 1996), especially pp. 114–83.

The Failure of Conflict Resolution in Cambodia: Causes and Lessons

David W. Ashley

Introduction

The coup d'état of July 5–6, 1997, finally brought home to a largely unsuspecting world the failure—or at the very least the failings—of the Cambodian peace process, long promoted as the most ambitious and successful of the various post–cold war attempts to settle protracted civil conflicts. This should provoke a reassessment of the international community's strategy for resolving such conflicts in general and international policy toward the Cambodian conflict in particular. This chapter seeks to contribute to such reassessment by exploring the strategy adopted to end the Cambodian civil war and the reasons for that strategy's ultimate failure. It does so by examining the collapse of the coalition government, the decline of the Khmer Rouge insurgency, and the response of the international community.

The Cambodian conflict, it must be remembered, should have been a relatively simple one to resolve. It was a dispute left over from the cold war, not a reaction to its end. It was not, fundamentally, a social, ethnic, or ideological conflict but rather a power struggle among Cambodian factions funded and supplied by various foreign patrons. The leaders' mutual hostility engendered by the recent past disguised a high degree of social homogeneity, popular war-weariness, and elite consensus about the way to run the country.

Cambodia also was a relatively easy place for the United Nations to begin its post–cold war peacemaking efforts. True, the country was simultaneously emerging from poverty, communism, and two decades of warfare that had devastated its human and physical resources. But it was manageably small, its factions were weak and heavily dependent on outside economic assistance, and an administrative apparatus existed to ensure a degree of peace and order over most of the country. The basic question was who should control the state—it was not, as in Afghanistan or Bosnia, whether a unitary, centralized state should exist at all. Finally, the UN began its work with the benefit of an almost unlimited mandate and a possibly unprecedented level of financial and political support from the international community.

In this context, efforts to resolve the Cambodian conflict took three basic forms: (1) international pressure, (2) liberalization, and (3) power sharing. This tripartite strategy achieved temporary success: An internationally acceptable coalition government was established; the Khmer Rouge was isolated and severely weakened; civil society took root; and international aid and investment fueled economic growth. By early 1996 many in the international donor community, their interest and resources waning, decided that the "Cambodia problem" had been resolved and turned their attention, with relief, to other countries.

Such confidence proved ill founded. Six years after the Paris Accords, the threat and reality of military force is once again the determining factor in Cambodian politics. Why? Because in the final analysis, power sharing as practiced in Cambodia was neither rooted in nor contributory to a genuine desire for reconciliation. The public move from the bullet to the ballot was not accompanied by the necessary efforts on the part of Cambodia's leaders to build the atmosphere and institutions that would have facilitated such a transformation. Peace and stability, instead of being founded on a political process incorporating debate and change, became contingent on the uneasy relationship of two unstable individuals, each of whom had meanwhile developed a private power base and one of whom had consistently used and threatened violence to further his political ends. Once that personal relationship collapsed in enmity, and Hun Sen's efforts to eliminate his opponent through political means failed, his resort to armed force was just a matter of time.

The Strategy to Achieve Peace

The three means used to effect conflict resolution were interlinked and, for the most part, mutually reinforcing. Of the three, the most important was international pressure. This comprised, on the one hand, the deinternationalization of the conflict by cutting off military and other assistance to the warring factions and, on the other, pledging aid and legitimacy to the government that resulted from the election. Since all the factions were totally reliant on outside financial and military support and lacked either power or legitimacy prior to 1991, they were particularly susceptible to the carrots and sticks of the international community.

Liberalization, economic and political, was a consequence of this international pressure. Anxious to end the war and its destabilizing impact on the region, the various foreign players pressured their clients to sign a commitment to switch from military to political struggle and to participate in an election that—given the inability of the factions to agree to an all-embracing coalition government—was the only available means to arrive at a legitimate administration. To facilitate the election, the Paris Accords guaranteed a liberal democracy and freedom of political action, association, and expression. The presence and actions of UNTAC then served to open up a space in which the competing political actors and members of the nascent civil society could operate. Numerous political parties, newspapers, and nongovernmental organizations (NGOs) sprang up.

At the same time, with the end to partisan foreign assistance, all factions had to open up to foreign trade and investment if they were to have the resources to survive. This, of course, took place in the context of the boom in the economies of Malaysia, Singapore, and Thailand, which caused them to be seriously interested for the first time in exploiting the economic opportunities available in their less-developed neighbors. As in Vietnam, Laos, and Burma, but in a more wide-ranging fashion, openness to foreign influence brought Cambodians new freedoms, new prosperity, and, of course, new problems.

Liberalization was not, however, the same as democratization; and pluralism was not the same as reconciliation. The factions agreed to the Paris Accords not because they were suddenly convinced of the values of peace and reconciliation but because—under heavy foreign pressure and with military victory out of reach—they had no choice. Likewise, they took part in the 1993 election not necessarily because of any enthusiasm for democracy; rather they hoped to achieve objectives (power or legitimacy) through the ballot box that they had failed to achieve on the battlefield. When the Khmer Rouge concluded that the election would damage rather than serve its interests, it sought to have the process scrapped in favor of its long-preferred option of a quadripartite coalition. But the other factions also saw the election not as a step toward reconciliation but as the latest, possibly decisive, stage in the war and fought it with corresponding violence.

This should not be surprising. Competitive elections—particularly when contested between former military adversaries—and national reconciliation are hardly obvious partners. To work, the game of democratic politics requires certain agreed rules. It demands a degree of mutual trust that all sides will play by those rules and a level of confidence that—win or lose—each party's most fundamental interests will be protected. It requires basic recognition of the legitimacy of one's competitors. In summary it must have certain institutions, traditions, and values that will serve to facilitate the political will of the victors while guaranteeing the legitimate rights of the losers. None of these were present in Cambodia.

These factors proved more decisive than the election results themselves in determining Cambodia's post-UNTAC future. When the results failed to reflect the administrative and military dominance of the Cambodian People's Party (CPP), they had to be shelved in favor of an intricate power-sharing arrangement between the CPP and the victorious royalist party, FUNCINPEC (the French acronym for the National United Front for an Independent, Neutral, Peaceful and Cooperative Cambodia). The CPP-FUNCINPEC alliance, first formed in 1991, was resurrected because it seemed, to many, the only realistic option. FUNCINPEC brought links with the West and democratic legitimacy as electoral victors; the ex-communist CPP brought institutional and military strength. For FUNCINPEC to go it alone would have risked a CPP coup; for the CPP to go it alone would have risked the international recognition and aid vital to sustaining the regime. The election results, in that sense, appeared perfect for the international community, for they strengthened FUNCINPEC's hand while forcing both parties to compromise.

The coalition government that emerged was thus acceptable to all the major international players and could be supported. This meant that for the international community the principal element of the conflict had been resolved as of mid-1993, and its efforts thereafter were concentrated on trying to consolidate and buttress the coalition government. This was the principal motivation behind the volume of foreign aid that flowed into the country after the elections and behind the donor nations' reluctance to condition or reduce that aid when problems began to emerge.

The Rise and Fall of the Coalition Government

Power Sharing: Flawed from the Start

Foreign assistance could not, however, ultimately compensate for the failure of the power-sharing arrangements. As noted above, by the early 1990s the conflict in Cambodia was not, at bottom, a fight over ethnic, social, or ideological differences but rather a struggle for power among factions—FUNCINPEC, the CPP and the Khmer Rouge. As no faction could eliminate the others militarily, peace depended on achieving a mutually acceptable political settlement among some or all of them. In the absence of genuine reconciliation and the willingness to abide by democratic norms, such a political settlement could be achieved only by sharing authority and roles within the unitary state. The division of ministries and military regions between parties is thus to Cambodia what, say, territorial division among ethnic groups is to Bosnia. Against this background the disputes over the division of power that emerged between the CPP and FUNCINPEC, particularly after 1996, could not be viewed as a healthy sign of democracy nor a normal facet of a coalition administration. Rather they constituted a severe threat to a largely unwritten cease-fire agreement.

A similar widely shared illusion was to see the coalition government as reflecting a desire for reconciliation and tolerance on the part of the two rival leaders. Instead it represented extreme distrust and an inability to compromise. The "consensus" principle, that all decisions of the royal government and its institutions were to be agreed to by both parties, enshrined this mutual suspicion and naturally inclined the system to gridlock. In particular it gave the incumbent party (the CPP) veto power over any actions that threatened its fundamental political, financial, or institutional interests, including any to reform the governmental system or to extend power sharing to the subprovincial or judicial structures. The government thus worked so long and insofar as Prince Ranariddh agreed not to threaten the CPP's interests.

This predicament came about because none of the institutions or traditions that should have strengthened the hand of the election winners—an impartial and effective bureaucracy, a unified army loyal to the government of the day, an independent judiciary, a history of peaceful transfer of power—were in place in 1993. (Even more worrying, none will be present at the time of the 1998 elections either.) What existed was firmly under the CPP's control. The options available to FUNCINPEC on winning the 1993 election were stark: it could have formed a coalition with the CPP and accepted limited access to state power or tried to assert its electoral mandate and face renewed civil war. The CPP's refusal and UNTAC's inability to depoliticize the state structure has thus been one of the defining factors in post-1993 Cambodia and perhaps more important than UNTAC's success in organizing the election itself. Indeed much of what has followed has been the logical outcome of UNTAC's failure to reform the state machinery and disarm and demobilize the factional armies. Like UNTAC, FUNCINPEC was to find it politically impossible to reform that machinery or demobilize the armies (although, admittedly, neither had clear plans nor made a systematic attempt to achieve these objectives). Like UNTAC, FUNCINPEC also was left with the choice of accepting the status quo or using its own distinct structure to achieve its goals.

The practical consequence of the continued CPP stranglehold over the state apparatus was that the only way FUNCINPEC could enforce its electoral mandate and (as important) reward its followers was to bring in and use its own people. This occurred not only at the ministerial level, as would be normal in a coalition government, but throughout the state system, in what was formally justified as a post-conflict "unification of existing administrative structures." This involved FUNCINPEC (and to a lesser extent the third participating faction, the Buddhist Liberal Democratic Party or BLDP) integrating small numbers of existing and large numbers of newly recruited civil servants, police, and military into the already bloated apparatus of the former CPP-controlled state of Cambodia. The two-party "consensus" system was extended to all state institutions. The distinction between party and government became virtually meaningless, and party (or factional) considerations almost always took precedence over governing for the benefit of the Cambodian people.

The result: Rather than depoliticizing a one-party state (controlled by the CPP), power sharing Cambodian-style created two separate and competing party states operating within every ministry, province, military command, and police commissariat. Instead of working with their counterparts from the other party, officials from the prime ministers level down conducted business with their party clients and colleagues. The power-sharing arrangements thus served to weaken the state by building and reinforcing parallel structures of personal and party authority, operating both within and outside the state. Hierarchical patron-client networks, a constant in Cambodian political history of radically changing regimes, have expanded and subsumed the formal state structure.

Most dangerously these parallel structures of authority also embraced the security forces—the military, police, and gendarmerie. The army was huge and undisciplined. Four years of a unified Royal Cambodian Armed Forces (RCAF) did little to weaken each unit's loyalty to its faction leaders—hardly surprising given that the co–prime ministers were also co–commanders-in-chief. The official pretense of a politically neutral security force was flagrantly violated by all sides. Even while some regular divisions of the RCAF under the control of General Ke Kim Yan, the moderate CPP chief of staff, largely stayed out of party squabbles, the same was never true of the police, gendarmerie, provincial armies, or militia, let alone the co-premiers' bodyguard units—all of which remained under partisan political control. Even when political conflicts were not an issue, the confused and competing chains of command of the numerous security units—combined with the financial interests of officers throughout the structure—led to frequent clashes between various elements of the "government's" forces.

The growth and consolidation of two major parallel structures of authority also affected the power relationships within the parties themselves. These parallel structures are ultimately determined by their respective leaders, Hun Sen and Prince Ranariddh, and have thus significantly bolstered the co–prime ministers' personal power in their parties. This is why the two men became so crucial to past stability and present instability. The dynamic has been especially important in the case of Hun Sen, who, suspicious of his CPP colleagues, has successfully sought to expand his independent scope for action. By using the phenomenal financial resources he managed to accumulate through his position as co-premier, Hun Sen constructed a formidable personal power base. This included building up client networks in the government, the bureaucracy, the RCAF, police, and gendarmerie as well as creating his own powerful media machine (several radio and television stations and over 20 newspapers), a large and powerful team of advisers (which increasingly acted as a shadow government), and a 1,500-man private army. Through his media outlets and his prominent development projects, he vigorously promoted his own image and popularity—separate from and frequently in competition with the rest of the CPP.

All this did not go without notice or criticism within Hun Sen's party—the elections in March 1997 for additional CPP Central Committee members proved a crushing defeat for his closest allies and showed the depth of internal distrust. But rather than make him toe the party line, this rebuff served to further the second prime minister's isolation from his party colleagues, who, afraid of his dictatorial tendencies and worried about international reaction, had consistently sought to restrain his more rash and aggressive actions. Hun Sen's ever-growing capacity and willingness to act alone, politically and militarily, is a key underlying cause of the political turmoil of 1997. It also makes it highly likely that Cambodian politics will remain unstable and bloody.

The Effects of the "Two Party States" System on Governance

Not surprisingly, the division of the state apparatus into separate and competing party structures had serious implications for the effectiveness of the government. This division was the primary reason that no serious attempt at structural reform began in any institution, despite frequent government pledges to the donor community to reduce the extremely overmanned army and civil service. As every official was considered someone's client and nominally loyal to one party or other, no retrenchment was possible without agreement between the parties as to the ultimate political character of the state. Without retrenchment, no progress could be made on increasing civil service wages to anything approaching realistic levels. And without proper wages, nothing could be done to eliminate the rampant corruption, inefficiency, and illdiscipline that permeates the civil service and military.

Politics frustrated more than the reform of the civil service. Any attempt to strengthen the state depended on finding additional sources of state revenue—at present heavily dependent on foreign aid and customs duties. Any serious attempt to do so, however, threatened the ability of the two parties to finance their power bases, which they did by exploiting the economic opportunities created by liberalization. The co–prime ministers' ability to reward their clients and build networks of patronage largely depended on diverting money from the state budget, either directly (as in the case of forestry or rubber revenues) or indirectly (by taking contributions in the form of money or shares from businessmen in exchange for tax exemptions or artificially low tax rates or turning a blind eye to criminal activities). This not only hurt the newly reconstituted state, it also weakened its position in the long term vis-à-vis a new sociopolitical elite.

The factionalization of the state also belied any governmental claim to be building the rule of law. Virtually all the laws passed by the National Assembly—on everything from prostitution and immigration to investment and pharmaceuticals, not to mention the constitution itself—were honored only in the breach. This was for two reasons. First, the institutions responsible for dissemination and implementation of laws were extremely weak, and usually weaker than the business or political networks they were up against. The judicial system in particular, a minuscule item in the government's budget, steadily lost any remaining public trust as a result of conspicuous corruption, injustice, and political partiality.

Second, patrons throughout the system—up to and including the co–prime ministers—considered the need to protect their clients to be more important than justice. Any wrongdoing, from incompetence and laziness to murder and drug trafficking, and even complicity in genocide, was considered subordinate to building up and protecting one's party and personal networks. Besides, the other side was doing things just as bad if not worse, and there was a proliferation of illegal activity. Each side believed it unfair to make an example of one of their clients. Politics, not the law, was paramount.

Similarly, since the co–prime ministers and their followers enjoyed complete power over the entire political system, there was no interest in building up independent state institutions to provide checks and balances. Hence the failure to establish the Supreme Council of Magistracy, Constitutional Council, and National Congress along with the refusal to grant power to existing institutions—the legislative, judiciary, or monarchy. King Sihanouk's ability to promote national reconciliation was always limited but ended definitively in early 1996 when Hun Sen treated him as an out-and-out rival rather than a potential ally or impartial referee. In the four years following the elections, the National Assembly never once used—nor was allowed to use—its rights to debate government policies, question ministers in full session, initiate legislation, or hold votes on any matter of contention between the two parties. Whenever it sought to do so—such as when the assembly president formally asked for a government explanation of its negotiations with the breakaway faction of the Khmer Rouge—the executive refused to cooperate. Despite a constitutional provision requiring the government to respond to parliamentarians' questions within seven days, most questions were never answered at all.

The Failure to Develop a Democratic Discourse

The failure of the National Assembly to carry out its constitutional role was also symptomatic of a more basic problem in Cambodian political culture: the unwillingness of the Cambodian elite to tolerate, much less engage in, substantive political debate. The fact and manner of Sam Rainsy's expulsion from the assembly, the lifting of Prince Sirivudh's parliamentary immunity, and most recently the replacement of Prince Ranariddh as first prime minister—each with careful avoidance of parliamentary debate—are striking examples of the inability of Cambodia's politicians to deal with differences of opinion. In fact, the ability of the Assembly and the Council of Ministers to convene, however irregularly, has depended on the avoidance of politically controversial discussions. The only alternatives presently available in Cambodian political discourse are to agree on everything and work together or to fight each other: There appears no middle way. Thus the coalition essentially collapsed once it was recognized that the two parties might have differing interests and opinions.

This observation may seem surprising to those impressed by the rapid proliferation of media outlets—television and radio stations and, particularly, newspapers—before the coup. But the choices made by the Khmer-language media never included reasoned consideration or discussion of the benefits of alternative policies or parties (in part because the two major parties exhibited no substantive policy differences). Instead the various media exclusively served one party or the other, or in schizophrenic fashion, broadcast the speeches and statements of both governing parties without comment, or kept their heads down and evaded any mention of politics. If not for the speeches and declarations of the co–prime ministers and their spokesmen or the Khmer-language services of foreign radio stations, the average Cambodian would know nothing about the most important political developments of the past four years.

Although most of the Khmer-language press was not directly controlled by one party or the other, it was not genuinely independent. Most newspapers received financing from one of the political leaders and his allies and promoted their position. Political debate through the press largely consisted of exchanging insults according to predetermined positions. The unremitting and frequently crude nature of these attacks revealed the continued lack of effective parameters—whether political, constitutional, legal, moral, or simply tasteful—that might have helped construct a democratic political discourse. The work of human rights organizations and political think tanks in seeking to build such a discourse has been praiseworthy and encouraging but of little practical or political import so far.

Much as the sheer size and vibrancy of the press helped to hide the absence of democratic forums, so the positive effects of continued openness blinded many foreign observers to the destructive side effects and eventual failure of power sharing. A combination of free market forces and extensive foreign aid brought clear signs of development and newly created prosperity; the integration of most of the Khmer Rouge army into the RCAF enhanced this by bringing peace to much of the countryside. The government's laissez-faire approach toward investors and donors also was extended to foreign and domestic NGOs, human rights associations, newspapers, and other sectors of civil society, making Cambodia, in many ways, a "free" country.

These freedoms reflected in part the legacy of the Paris Accords and UNTAC, the government's reliance on foreign aid and investment as well as the reluctant acceptance—if not always tolerance— of diverse opinions. In many sectors foreign aid and NGOs either filled the gaps left by the state or funded and mobilized the government apparatus to act. In other instances, the state was too weak to check the new freedoms even when it wished to—such as with the opposition press or demonstrations—and politicians were thus forced to accept them or use occasional violence to try to keep them in check.

The extent of openness was a double-edged sword, however. It was in the context of uncontrolled liberalization, weak law-enforcement institutions, and the need of both parties to accumulate resources and protect their people at any cost that activities such as land grabbing, deforestation, and violent crime flourished. Rampant corruption, too, was both a cause and effect of these conditions. The weakness of the state, and the lack of interest from the powers that were, meant that both good and bad effects of liberalization enjoyed the same, benign official indifference. Most activities in Cambodia—economic, social, even political—occupied the same semi-legal, semi-illegal status. The freedom with which ideas, technology, and goods crossed national borders also facilitated the trafficking of drugs or nine-year-old Vietnamese girls to work as prostitutes in Phnom Penh. The freedom for someone to occupy public land undisturbed for 17 years accordingly allowed the local commune chief to forcibly evict him one day and sell the land to an investor. What should have been the postliberalization stage, namely the bounding of such freedoms by a rule of law, failed to come about. For any postcommunist state, this transition from controlling freedoms to safeguarding them is a difficult one. In Cambodia the political situation made the transition almost impossible, thus making it even harder for the country to deal with the social problems inevitably accompanying liberalization.

The Collapse of the Ruling Coalition

The de facto end of the FUNCINPEC-CPP coalition in 1996–97 along with the remilitarization of the Cambodian conflict was nei-. ther predetermined, nor surprising. The coalition had masked fundamental problems, and its survival was contingent upon factors, particularly the relationship between two volatile individuals. While the three factors promoting peace—international pressure, liberalization, and power sharing—effectively killed the Khmer Rouge as a coherent political force, they failed to have the same effect on the other factions. Power sharing served to bolster the rivalry between the principal parties—the CPP and FUNCINPEC—rather than encouraged reconciliation. In the context of economic liberalization, those parties with access to power were able to create and build up financial, and hence political, bases independent of ex–foreign patrons. Their vulnerability to international pressure, though still significant, thus declined slightly compared to 1991. While the viability and interests of both parties depended on continued openness to the global economy and a modicum of stability, their political interests were distinct and, by 1996, largely competing.

The consensus arrangement worked until early 1996 because the co-premiers managed to concentrate power in their hands and cooperate. In particular Prince Ranariddh agreed to put to one side the election results to govern on a formally equal basis with Hun Sen. Under the coalition formula, the consent of both parties (and ultimately both prime ministers) was required for any decision, and contentious issues—including those on which FUNCINPEC had campaigned, such as corruption and immigration—were not raised. This meant significant concessions on the part of Ranariddh: For the sake of the coalition and for his own political interests, he acquiesced in fighting and then outlawed the Khmer Rouge, sidelined his father, King Sihanouk, and discarded other electoral pledges. In their place he concentrated on the common concerns of his co-premier, such as promoting foreign relations and economic, social, and infrastructural development, at the same time bolstering their power and wealth along with that of their clients. For nearly three years the two men enthusiastically promoted a joint program of economic liberalism and political conservatism.

Prince Ranariddh was able to make this transformation almost overnight because FUNCINPEC was, arguably, less a political party with a clear political program than a royal court (in which the prince was surrounded by a small coterie of courtiers) interested in recreating the symbols and structures of the pre-1970 period. Internally Ranariddh dominated, and access to power and wealth was more important than ideology to all but FUNCINPEC's most politicized leaders. The sacking and subsequent expulsion of the most outspoken member of this small minority, Sam Rainsy, symbolized Ranariddh's willingness to eliminate any challenge to his decision to compromise with the CPP. Rainsy's Khmer Nation Party (KNP) has become another in the long line of breakaway movements from FUNCINPEC over the years.

Since policy issues were never crucial to the FUNCINPEC-CPP

relationship, its eventual fracture was over power not policies. In particular it was the result of immediate and potential threats to the power-sharing arrangement: the increasingly obvious imbalance in strength between the two prime ministers and their parties as well as the impending elections that spelled the end of the co-premier system. The spark was the November 1995 arrest of Prince Sirivudh, FUNCINPEC secretary-general and former foreign minister (and Sam Rainsy's most prominent ally within the party). Despite Prince Ranariddh's consent to the arrest, the incident clearly revealed Hun Sen's power as well as his hostility toward the royal family. The loss of the party secretary-general, combined with the approach of the 1998 elections, also meant that Ranariddh had to come to terms with the weakness of his party organization and the disillusionment among the party's membership at his failure to capitalize on the election victory.

At the FUNCINPEC Congress of March 1996—the first time Prince Ranariddh addressed a nationwide meeting of FUNCINPEC activists since the 1993 election—Ranariddh finally expressed his party's frustrations at the unequal nature of the coalition. He especially criticized the CPP's alleged refusal to share power at the district level (the aspect of power sharing of most interest to party activists); he also raised, for the first time since the 1993 election, the issue of Vietnamese domination that had been the raison d'être of FUNCINPEC's creation and the decade-long military struggle. His comments triggered a fierce reaction from Hun Sen, and the personal relationship that had sought stability was transformed into a major source of insecurity.

Having been Hun Sen's ally for nearly three years, Prince Ranariddh became the latest target—after the Khmer Rouge, Sam Rainsy, Son Sann, and Prince Sirivudh—of Hun Sen's ceaseless attempts to isolate and destroy his enemies. Ranariddh probably had been the ultimate target all along. From March 1996 Hun Sen appeared determined to force Ranariddh into either abject submission or into acting on his threat to withdraw from the government. Hun Sen tried various means: He rejected any further concessions on the issue of power sharing; he tried to undermine Ranariddh's control of FUNCINPEC by seeking to encourage an internal revolt against the royals and the overseas Khmer who dominated the party; he sought to ban royalty and Cambodians with dual nationality from standing in elections. Aware that hopes for peace and its relationship with the Khmer Rouge and the king were the principal cards FUNCINPEC might play in the local and national elections then scheduled for 1997 and 1998, Hun Sen tried to establish his own credentials as peacemaker while seeking to divide and weaken the Khmer Rouge and using his press outlets to attack King Sihanouk at every opportunity.

Both parties sought to bolster themselves in preparation for elections or renewed war, which neither side appeared to want. They competed to reconcile with each and every political actor, including the most minor political parties and newspapers and—not least, of course—the Khmer Rouge. For FUNCINPEC national reconciliation meant returning to the populist, anti-CPP rhetoric of pre-1993 and embracing its former allies in the KNP, BLDP, and—it hoped—the Khmer Rouge in the newly established National United Front. For Hun Sen reconciliation involved exploiting internal differences within the Front, so as to bring as many people over to his side as possible. His tactics were often successful. With the reduced relevance of post-1979 ideological stereotypes and the greater importance of money politics, it became easier to dissolve old political alliances and build new ones. Personal friendships and enmities within the country's small political elite, some long-standing and some newly developed, combined with ambition and greed to become greater determinants of political alignments than pre-1993 factional labels.

Nonetheless, despite all his new friends, Hun Sen was making too many enemies and eliminating too few of them. By March 1997 Hun Sen's strategy of divide and rule was facing a serious threat: A National United Front evolved mainly by being anti–Hun Sen. According to rumors widely circulated and given credence in Phnom Penh, CPP opinion polls were confirming the widespread unpopularity of Hun Sen (which was evident to any casual visitor to Cambodia who bothered to speak to ordinary people) and the potential electoral appeal of a FUNCINPEC-KNP-BLDP alliance. His previous attempts at intimidating, splitting, framing, and defaming his opponents having failed, Hun Sen turned to more drastic measures. The barbaric March 30 grenade attack on a lawful KNP demonstration in front of the symbol of democracy, the National Assembly—which is thought to have been organized and carried out with the complicity of Hun Sen's bodyguard—was the defining moment. It demonstrated that, henceforth, Hun Sen would stop at nothing to protect his power.

Two weeks later, coinciding with his intense preparations for military action in the face of the expected return of Prince Sirivudh, Hun Sen personally orchestrated a split in FUNCINPEC by openly providing financial, political, media, and security support to a small breakaway faction whose sole aim was to end the National United Front and dismiss Prince Ranariddh as first prime minister.[1] When this ploy failed, because Hun Sen could not attain the necessary two-thirds majority in the National Assembly, he reverted to force to achieve the same goals.

Beginning on July 2 forces personally loyal to Hun Sen began implementing a well-organized plan to forcibly disarm troops loyal to FUNCINPEC in Phnom Penh. The aim of this unilateral military action, as Hun Sen stated publicly on July 5, was to dismiss and replace Ranarridh. The pretext (the only one he ever could have offered) was, of course, the Khmer Rouge: that Ranariddh had brought thousands of soldiers from Anlong Veng into Phnom Penh in an attempt to stage a coup and bring back the "genocidal regime." In fact, although former Khmer Rouge were fighting on both sides on July 5–6, the total number of "hard-line" Khmer Rouge produced after the coup as evidence of Ranariddh's plot was one 16-year-old boy.[2] In reality, at the exact time of Hun Sen's actions, Pol Pot was under house arrest and the Khmer Rouge was in its weakest position, politically and militarily, in 30 years.

The Demise of the Khmer Rouge

It is deeply ironic, but far from coincidental, that the Khmer Rouge and the ruling coalition should fall apart at precisely the same time. Disguised as efforts toward national reconciliation, both Hun Sen's and Prince Ranarridh's quest to achieve political, military, and propaganda advantages associated with allying with as many individuals and groups as possible had a contradictory and unpredictable effect on the Khmer Rouge. The post-1993 isolation and decline of Pol Pot's guerrilla movement had been the most striking success of the coalition government and the international community. Thus, at one level, the rivalry that commenced after March 1996 for the Khmer Rouge's attentions brought new political possibilities for an increasingly weak and marginal force. At another level, however, the competition ended up engendering a series of deeply damaging splits within the Khmer Rouge. As the last Maoist movement in Southeast Asia, the Khmer Rouge already had little future, but the events of 1996–97 served, on balance, to shorten this last chapter in the movement's bloody history.[3]

That chapter had begun with the Paris Accords. The Khmer Rouge, or Partie of Democratic Kampuchea (PDK), had agreed to the 1991 settlement in part under heavy Chinese pressure but also in the hope of improving its position. Pol Pot, the undisputed strategist of the movement, expected that a combination of a large UN presence and a quadripartite Sihanouk-led "super-government" (i.e., the Supreme National Council) would severely weaken the PDK's principal enemy, the CPP. In particular he felt that the peace process could advance the Khmer Rouge's long-standing attempts to dismantle the local-level state apparatus of the CPP regime. Meanwhile a PDK role at all levels of a pre- and post-election state would, Pol Pot believed, have two very positive consequences. On the one hand, it would make the PDK a legitimate participant in the political process. On the other it would give it the capacity to defend its territory, economy, population, forces, and leadership from the inevitable dangers that embracing capitalism and power sharing would bring. The Khmer Rouge would thus be able to survive the loss of foreign assistance by building up a domestic economic, political, and military powerbase. Then, at some moment, the Khmer Rouge would use this powerbase as a springboard to regain power through political or military means; perhaps much as the Lao and South Vietnamese communists had done two years after the Paris Accords of 1973.

Shortly after the October 1991 peace settlement, however, the PDK leaders significantly revised their analysis and decided instead that the UN presence was going to bolster, rather than undermine, the CPP state structure. Pol Pot saw the November 1991 alliance of CPP and FUNCINPEC as a Western-inspired arrangement to isolate the Khmer Rouge and convert the Paris Accords into an alternative bipartite settlement. The events of 1992 and 1993 only served to confirm his faith in this analysis. In response the Khmer Rouge opted out of participating in the 1993 elections and banned UNTAC personnel from the areas under its control. Pol Pot saw

UNTAC's failure to dismantle the CPP state apparatus and the subsequent establishment of the "two-headed" coalition government as a Western attempt to legitimize the "Vietnamese puppet" regime the Khmer Rouge had fought for 15 years.

To accept "peace" and give up territorial, organizational, and military strength while the CPP retained administrative control of the country would, Pol Pot believed, be akin to suicide. He thus concluded by mid-1994 that the Khmer Rouge had no choice but to continue a potentially endless military struggle. But their ability to do so was greatly weakened by the combined effect of international pressure, liberalization, and power sharing.

First the loss of foreign material and logistical support seriously affected the PDK's military strength. The Paris Accords and subsequent international pressure on Thailand to end its links with the Khmer Rouge left the latter on its own for the first time. With no hope of short-term victory over a far larger enemy and facing difficulties in purchasing and bringing adequate ammunition across the Thai border, the movement reverted to a "prolonged war" using 1960s-style tactics and self-made "traditional weapons." With such means they could generally defend their base areas but lost almost all offensive capability. As in the 1960s an isolated guerrilla movement posed no serious threat to the regime in Phnom Penh. The post-election period thus saw a gradual but significant reduction in the potency and geographical reach of the PDK's military threat. Cadres at all levels of the movement could not help but conclude that the armed struggle was going nowhere.

Second the temporary embrace of political and economic liberalization severely undermined the Khmer Rouge. In spite of initial delusions to the contrary, the PDK was far less capable than the other factions of transforming itself into a political party. Its structure, thinking, and leadership were outdated and inflexible. Its appeal was rooted in an anti-Vietnamese nationalist message whose potency steadily declined after the Vietnamese troop withdrawal in 1989. Its ideological and organizational coherence had been based on the paranoid isolation of its troops and population base from the outside world. The temporary exposure to freedoms of trade, movement, religion, property, and—not least—peace and normalcy sapped the will to fight among the vast majority of the PDK.

Recognizing the problem, in mid-1994 Pol Pot withdrew all the freedoms granted since 1991 as well as the moderate "united front" policies in place since 1979. In their stead he reintroduced the brutal class-struggle rhetoric, discipline, and tactics that the movement, supposedly, had definitively renounced. The effect, unsurprisingly, was to deepen the disillusionment felt by many Khmer Rouge cadres and combatants.

Third the post-election power-sharing arrangements meant that the Khmer Rouge had lost not only their international friends but also their domestic united front allies; their former battlefield comrades were now their battlefield foes. This not only directly weakened their military and political prospects but also gave many in the PDK the confidence and the contacts to negotiate defections.

It was a combination of all these developments that led to the potentially fatal split in the Khmer Rouge. In mid-1996, disillusioned with the revived hard-line tactics and an unending, unwinnable war, leading cadres in the two major bases in the northwest rejected both orders to take additional property under collective control and the leader, Son Sen, who had been locally assigned to enforce them locally. When the highest leadership backed Son Sen rather than the rebels, the insurrection rapidly transformed from one against a specific order and leader to one against the movement.

One additional factor, however, had to be in place before the entire Khmer Rouge army in the west—however unhappy with their old leadership— would agree to a cease-fire and join the government forces. Ironically while international pressure, liberalization, and power sharing were crucial to the schism in the Khmer Rouge, that split would not have occurred had it not been for the growing tensions within the ruling coalition in Phnom Penh. The rivalry between Ranarridh and Hun Sen led both to court the Khmer Rouge—dissidents and hard-liners, before and after the revolt. Each offered attractive terms—continued control of armies, resources, and territory, senior military or civilian positions for PDK officers, amnesty for the political éminence grise of the rebellion, and so forth. These terms were not on the negotiating table in 1993–94 when the coalition was solid. The upshot was that the movement fractured: Differing political preferences, personal animosities, conflicting ambitions, and contrary financial interests temporarily proved more important than the joint legacy of a decades-long struggle. Some Khmer Rouge elements joined the CPP and FUNC-

INPEC, while those in the heartland of the August 1996 rebellion—in the towns of Pailin and Malai—successfully safeguarded their autonomy and neutrality.

As for the few remaining hard-line PDK forces, by 1997, they were limited to a few northern and northeastern provinces and almost entirely occupied with defending their last significant base, Anlong Veng. The same factors that had led to the widespread defections and breakaways since the elections, however, continued to undermine even this last stronghold. The additional questions of who was to blame for the disastrous decline of the movement and how to deal with that decline dogged the leadership, as did the perennial issue of succession. Pushed to answer these fundamental questions by FUNCINPEC's increasingly urgent offers of a more-or-less overt alliance, the remaining senior leadership collapsed in enmity. Pol Pot tried one last purge against his long-time comrade and military commander, Ta Mok, but did not have the necessary forces to carry it through. Since moving to Anlong Veng in late 1993 he had been almost entirely dependent on Ta Mok's military strength. Instead Ta Mok and his followers took over, and Pol Pot and his favored commanders were captured, put under house arrest, and divested of their political influence. (Pol Pot died on April 15, 1998, at the age of 73, while still under house arrest in northern Cambodia.)

Freed of Pol Pot's dogmatic leadership and exploiting the political advantage brought by his arrest, the remaining Khmer Rouge were able to join FUNCINPEC in an alliance that sought to bolster Prince Ranariddh militarily and politically in the face of the imminent armed threat posed by Hun Sen. The change in Anlong Veng—the removal of major personal and political causes behind the 1996 split, although not the central question of war or peace—also created the possibility of a realignment of the various former Khmer Rouge elements in the west. If FUNCINPEC's aim had been to intimidate Hun Sen into inaction, it failed. Hun Sen had already decided on military action, and, if anything, the possibility that Ranariddh might now pose as the agent of justice, peace, and national reconciliation while strengthening FUNCINPEC's military forces made such action seem even more urgent. Less than one month after Ta Mok's military coup, Hun Sen staged his own.

The Role of the International Community

By early 1997 the competing ambitions and mutual animosities of the co-premiers made the continued existence of the power-sharing coalition highly uncertain. Cambodia's highly vaunted "political stability" became less and less sustainable. Elections were scheduled to be held in 1998, but the complete lack of trust between the only two men who really counted undermined any attempt to organize the elections or reach any alternative political settlement. One alternative would have been to reach an agreement to continue the coalition indefinitely, but given the mutual animosity (and the constitutional requirement that the two-premier system cease after 1998), this was impossible. At the same time, neither Hun Sen nor Prince Ranarridh was prepared to rely on elections to determine the next government. The political and financial stakes were too high. Without any precedent in Cambodian history for a peaceful transition of power, both sides viewed the elections with the hope of absolute victory and fear of total defeat, with no a priori limits to either. Since no progress had been made in creating a rule of law or building democratic institutions, the only way to protect one's wealth and position was to hold onto power. These hopes and fears, as well as the weaknesses of the state and civil society, made both factions more interested in preparing to win the elections than in taking the legal and administrative steps required to hold them fairly.

Nonetheless the resort to weapons was not inevitable. The same factors that had made large segments of the Khmer Rouge leadership and army demand peace in late 1996 also were acting on the two ruling parties. Neither party, as opposed to particular individuals, actively wanted renewed warfare. Indeed recognizing the popular yearning to end the war, both parties wanted to appear as the architects of peace. Though the leaders' authority remained supreme, there was war weariness among party ranks as well as among the electorate—a sentiment that was strikingly evident in the widespread anger with Hun Sen following the July coup. The extent of official corruption meant senior figures of both parties had much to lose, as well as much to gain, from further fighting. Each party, too, was constrained by fear of the other's strength and ability to fight back. Like the Khmer Rouge, both had men and weapons, but neither, particularly FUNCINPEC, had the ammunition and logistical capacity to sustain a prolonged war.

The International Community and the July Coup

Above all both sides were acutely aware of the international community's position. Both knew that Cambodia would continue to be reliant on foreign investment and international aid for the foreseeable future. Although they were stronger than they had been a few years earlier, both were still susceptible to the financial need and resultant international pressure that helped produce temporary resolutions of the Cambodian conflict in 1991 and 1993.

By July 1997 two things had changed that made all the difference. First Hun Sen was willing to ignore the concerns of his CPP colleagues and the general population. Second he perceived an altered international attitude toward the "Cambodia problem." Tired of a nonsensical, factional squabble in a small and strategically insignificant country, and frustrated that its "success" in securing the Paris Accords and the 1993 election proved short-lived, the international community had little desire to continue peacekeeping in Cambodia. This attitude, evident throughout the diplomatic corps in Phnom Penh and at the United Nations, was crucial because, since more power sharing and liberalization could not achieve peace, international pressure was the only thing standing between Cambodia and renewed conflict.

In the crucial months of April to June 1997, an imaginative, principled, coordinated, and proactive international approach—whether led by the major donors, the UN, or the Association of Southeast Asian Nations (ASEAN)—still could have rescued the peace process into which the so many lives and so much time, money, and effort had been invested. The trouble was that the requisite foresight, imagination, principles, and leadership were singularly lacking. The only thing offered, whenever erupting violence forced some fleeting international response, were empty platitudes and toothless appeals to the goodwill of leaders who, all evidence suggested, had none. The UN Security Council paid no attention to Cambodia. The appeal made by the U.S., Japan and other industrialized nations at the "Group of Eight" meeting on June 22 was the strongest expression of international concern, but any impact was rapidly undermined by a series of seemingly uncoordinated visits by "special envoys" of different countries, each failing to address the root causes of the problem. The last-minute cancellation of U.S. secretary of state Madeleine Albright's scheduled visit on June 27 gave the strong impression that the United States had no policy toward, and little interest in, the country. The donor countries, meeting in Paris only days before the coup, had little inkling of what was unfolding.

But the failure of the international community was a matter of years, not days. Hun Sen—the only political player with the means, motive, and desire to take decisive military action—calculated that the international appeals to refrain from violence would not be supported by any concerted action because of all he had seen of the major international players over the previous four or more years. Ever since his experience during the UNTAC period, Hun Sen had considered the international community a paper tiger. As he continually and skillfully sought to protect and expand his personal power, he reckoned on the failure of the international community, particularly the donors, to match its rhetoric with action. He believed that, whatever the requirements of the Paris Accords, the outside players were interested only in the facade of democracy—i.e., in a coalition government and elections irrespective of content—and were willing to turn a blind eye to almost any abuse of the principles of democracy and human rights in the name of stability. Clearly this belief underpinned his move against Prince Ranariddh in July. And to a large extent, he has been proved right.

With the partial and important exceptions of the United States and ASEAN, the international community has done little to oppose the July coup d'état. Western countries such as France, Canada, and Australia have remained oblivious to the use of force to usurp an elected prime minister, apparently in the hope that the coup will bring stability. They are right if they thought that the power-sharing experiment was failing and that Prince Ranariddh was an ineffective, unprincipled politician. Yet for Ranariddh's many faults, he was not the one who abused his power as a co–commander in chief to attack his co–prime minister. And he was not the one who went on television in fatigues on the morning of July 5, when hardly a shot had been fired, and declared his intention to use military force to dismiss his counterpart and unilaterally change the government.

The countries that accepted the July 1997 coup and are preparing to accept potentially noncompetitive elections in 1998 are profoundly wrong if they think that Hun Sen's dominant position will produce stability. Coups d'état, wherever they occur, have a nasty habit of repeating themselves. The events of July 5–6 will only further postpone the day when Cambodia will be able to deal with its political conflicts through peaceful and democratic means. Moreover, any hope that Hun Sen, having vanquished Prince Ranariddh, will henceforth preside over a stable and efficient, if slightly authoritarian, administration is based on a total misreading of his personality. Once FUNCINPEC, the KNP, and the BLDP have been destroyed as potential challengers, it is highly probable that Hun Sen will move against his next set of rivals—those within the CPP—and will continue to employ violence whenever he deems it necessary.

While some countries are prepared to forgo principles and provide Hun Sen unconditional backing, others are looking to the 1998 elections as a means to finally resolve the Cambodian conflict. They are pushing for a cease-fire and minimally fair elections as a way to solve the current crisis and establish a legitimate government. While these are admirable objectives, they ignore the lessons of the past five years. Conflicts in nations like Cambodia, Haiti, or Sierra Leone are deep-rooted, emanating from failings in their political culture and development; achieving sustainable peace and democracy requires more than just arranging a cease-fire between factions and organizing elections. Elections alone are not going to eradicate the poisonous animosity, distrust, and rapaciousness that characterize Cambodia's political elite. Likewise, it may be possible to achieve stability in some conflict-ridden countries by establishing power-sharing arrangements among rival factions or legitimizing the dominance of one of them, but such stability is likely to be short-term and fragile unless accompanied by the growth of institutions, values, and traditions that foster political debate, encourage compromise, and ensure a degree of accountability.

It is by promoting the development of these institutions, values, and traditions—the underpinnings of constitutional liberalism—that the international community will help to finally end the Cambodian conflict. Such a strategy does not mean taking sides, but nor does it mean giving up basic principles in the search for a quick and easy solution. What the strategy does mean is promoting agreement among all parties on necessary reforms to achieve a professional, politically neutral, and properly resourced bureaucratic and judicial structure. It also means promoting constitutional changes that reduce the importance of executive power, thus ending the overriding importance of any one election. And it means vigorously condemning and taking concerted action against events and individuals that contravene peace, human rights, and democracy.

The Challenge of Bringing Justice to Cambodia

Finally a strategy for achieving a lasting peace and democracy in Cambodia must also include an effort on the part of Cambodians and the international community to address the continuing absence of accountability and justice. When the Paris Accords were negotiated in 1990–91, the issue of "transitional justice" was deliberately avoided. Ensuring the participation of the Chinese, Thais, and Khmer Rouge in a comprehensive peace settlement was considered more important than accountability for the gross crimes of the 1970s and 1980s. The human rights provisions in the accords looked to the future rather than to the past: They were concerned with preventing the return of the "policies and practices of the past" rather than punishing their perpetrators.

Whether this choice was right or wrong, the world and Cambodia have moved on. The events in the former Yugoslavia and Rwanda forced the international community to look again at the issues of civil war, genocide, and justice. The end of the cold war also meant that, in newly democratic countries throughout Africa, Asia, Latin America, and Eastern Europe, people looked for ways to deal with the legacy of dictatorship and abuse so as to achieve justice, promote reconciliation, bring closure, and prevent future abuses. The issue in most afflicted countries has become how, not whether, to confront the horrors of the past.

Events in Cambodia, too, have made it both necessary and possible to confront the issue of accountability. To begin with, any hope that a new page could be turned and that the past could be forgotten has been disproved by events. In choosing peace over justice Cambodians and the international community have failed to achieve either. Political violence, and impunity for its agents, is still the norm in Cambodia and continues to be both the cause and effect of the continuing crisis. Equally important, the military decline, diplomatic isolation, and near-fatal split in the Khmer Rouge have brought new possibilities. The demise of the Khmer Rouge suggested, for the first time, that it may be possible to arrest and bring to trial the individuals bearing greatest responsibility for one of the darkest periods in human history. Indeed, at one point in June 1997 and again prior to his death, Pol Pot might have been thrust into the hands of an international community completely at a loss as to what to do with him. (Only the United States has shown any real interest, however belated, in pursuing an issue that most governments appear happy to consign to the history books.)

At the same time, however, the old, practical obstacles to bringing senior Khmer Rouge leaders to justice largely have been replaced by new, political ones. Domestically the leaders of both the CPP and FUNCINPEC have proved willing to enthusiastically embrace, for their own political gain, persons suspected of having committed crimes against humanity both before and after 1979. Neither ethical nor legal considerations have prevented the rehabilitation of notorious leaders and lesser-known but more obviously culpable military and security figures. So long as elements of the present and former Khmer Rouge remain useful allies for one side or the other in the Cambodian conflict, the search for real justice will remain difficult and prolonged.

It is, ultimately, the right and duty of the Cambodian people to choose how they wish to come to terms with their past. Unfortunately, given the current political situation and, more fundamentally, the absence of any channels for democratic discourse, nothing remotely akin to South Africa's wide-ranging debate has taken place—or is likely to take place—within Cambodia as to what form accountability should take. Decisions that ideally should be made by Cambodians will have to be left to outsiders. The June 1997 decision of the two prime ministers, whatever their reasons, to request UN assistance to bring to justice those responsible for the 1975–79 atrocities was an extremely welcome first step. It finally gives the international community the opportunity and duty to deal in a proper judicial manner with the crimes against humanity that have taken place in Cambodia: Evidence, not politics, can determine who is indicted and punished.

The members of the UN must respond positively to Cambodia's request. The issue of past crimes against humanity in Cambodia cannot be considered an internal problem for four reasons. First given the marked political bias and chronic lack of human and financial resources available in the Cambodian court system, any credible mechanism for investigating, acknowledging, and punishing the crimes of the past will inevitably require substantial external support, both financial and technical. Second those crimes cannot be divorced from the context of war and peace, both of which foreign players were instrumental in bringing about. Third if the issue of past human rights violations is not dealt with in a proper judicial manner, it will continue to bedevil the political and electoral process the international community seeks to promote. The bloodshed on both sides will be used as an excuse to continue the killing. Who is blamed and punished for the continued killings will depend on who wins or loses politically—not on who is guilty. This is not only unjust but destabilizing, for it only adds to the overriding importance of staying in power. Fourth and most important, the human rights abuses in Cambodia over the past 25 years are of a nature and scale that constitute crimes under international as well as domestic law. Other countries have not just a right, but an absolute moral and legal obligation to help bring those responsible to justice.

The only question facing the UN thus should be how, not whether, to carry out this obligation. The principal options are a truth commission or criminal tribunal. Although a truth commission can serve a useful function, only an international criminal tribunal can fulfill the need for justice and end the cycle of violence and impunity in Cambodia.

The problem in Cambodia is not—as it was in, say, Chile or Argentina—that past crimes have not been officially acknowledged. Indeed, for 14 years, the Cambodian people heard about little else but the crimes of the "genocidal Pol Pot clique." Rather the problem is that no one has ever been tried and punished for these horrific and widely known crimes and the country's leaders embrace, deal with, or are commonly believed to be those responsible for the genocide. This being the case, how can respect for the law ever be engendered? (Practically the only exceptions to this are high-level political and security figures who have been arrested and tried for political reasons—such blatant unfairness only brings the law into further disrepute.)

Against this background a truth commission on the events of 1975–79 appears insufficient: The truth is too well-known, and the crimes are too severe. While a truth commission may be a simpler and politically more acceptable option, any process identifying people culpable of mass-murder or genocide that does not lead to punishment will only undermine faith in the rule of law further. Instead what is needed is an example of a scrupulously fair trial leading to the punishment of those responsible, however politically significant or utterly insignificant they may be today. This would achieve justice for the past victims of the Khmer Rouge and contribute to a rule of law for the future. To achieve these purposes, the mandate and conduct of the trial must be based on legal and ethical considerations only—that is, to bring to justice all those legally culpable for the commission of crimes against humanity, not to indict any particular individual or political grouping. In present circumstances only an international tribunal will suffice.[4]

The question of accountability for the crimes of the 1970s cannot be divorced from the problem of contemporary impunity—the de facto and sometimes de jure freedom of those with power, money, or weapons to conduct all kinds of illegal activity without fear of prosecution. Any move to bring to trial those responsible for old crimes not accompanied by measures to end impunity for more recent violations will be looked on with bemusement by many Cambodians. There is little point in dealing with the horrific crimes of 20 years ago when atrocities of a similar nature if not scale continue. The international court should, therefore, have a mandate and the resources to investigate all violations of international humanitarian law that have taken place from 1975 to the present. The court should have the independent power to decide which cases to investigate and make those decisions based on the severity of the crime and the availability of evidence. Of course an international tribunal is only a partial response to a more fundamental problem: Cambodia lacks a judicial system with the capacity, prestige, and independence needed to end impunity. Therefore it is important that an international tribunal be structured to strengthen, not replace, the national system of justice.

If established alongside, rather than instead of, an international court, a truth commission can play an important complementary role. It can achieve certain things that a tribunal cannot. As East Germany has demonstrated, tribunals are not always the best way to approach the broader social and institutional questions of why abuses occur and why criminal regimes last. No one in Cambodia needs to be told that the Khmer Rouge committed serious crimes. What is lacking in Cambodia, ever since 1979, is a discussion of the real causes of those crimes and the responsibility of Cambodians in perpetrating them. This is not limited to the "Pol Pot period." Despite human rights abuses having occurred continuously over at least the last 30 years, no political actor, from whatever faction, has ever apologized or been punished by his own side for his role in such abuses. No unit responsible for political violence, ethnic killings, or a myriad of other illegal activities has ever been dismantled; no commander ever made to explain, justify, or repent his actions. No debate has ever taken place as to why abuses occurred and are allowed to continue. Everyone affirms a commitment to "human rights" and "multiparty liberal democracy," but no one explains what was wrong with their former beliefs or why it is only now that they have "seen the light."

The aim of a truth commission would be not so much to reveal the nature or extent of those crimes (although this certainly needs to be undertaken for future generations and the prevention of politically motivated historical revisionism), but to provoke a wider debate and understanding about the causes and legacies of the Khmer Rouge regime. To achieve its purpose, the commission would have to be properly resourced and strictly impartial. Both these requirements mean, unfortunately, that the commission probably would have to be established and staffed, at least in part, by non-Cambodians. Its success, however, would depend on achieving and retaining broad international and domestic support of its activities and findings. More important, it would have to find a way—through its mode of working and disseminating its results—to provoke debate and an internal reckoning among a largely uneducated society.

Unfortunately neither a tribunal nor a truth commission is a shortcut to justice, truth, democracy, peace, or reconciliation. As in other countries, a successful attempt to deal with the past is far more likely to be a result than a cause of a successful transition. The establishment of a truth commission, unlike that of an international court, may have to await a political environment in which findings would be seriously considered and acted upon by the Cambodian government of the day. We may have to wait a long time.

The path to resolving longstanding conflicts will never be short or trouble free, and boredom, fatigue, or disappointment are not good reasons to give up halfway. The role of the international community in Cambodia remains critical. The signatories of the Paris Accords must accept that they have a continued, legal obligation toward the country. If it was worth devoting $2 billion and, more important, the lives of several dozen UN personnel for peace in Cambodia in 1991–92, then surely it is worth spending a little more time and effort now.

Notes

1. The full extent of Hun Sen's role was revealed to the author in a series of interviews in April–May 1997 with FUNCINPEC members involved, or asked to participate, in the breakaway group.

2. This boy, Phy Ra, had been brought by General Nhiek Bun Chhay, the commander of FUNCINPEC forces, from Anlong Veng some weeks before the coup and reportedly did housework at the general's home. No evidence of the presence of any other "hard-line" Khmer Rouge was ever produced by Hun Sen's faction. The in-depth investigation by the Cambodia office of the UN Centre for Human Rights into persons detained and killed during and after the coup identified no known Khmer Rouge among them.

3. These events are described and analyzed in greater depth in David Chandler, "Living Out the Death of the Khmer Rouge, 1993–96." (Paper presented at a conference on Cambodia: Power, Myth, and Memory, Monash University, Australia, December 1996).

4. The issue of what sort of international tribunal and how it should be set up is too complex to be dealt with here. The options are discussed in Jason S. Abrams and Steven R. Ratner, "Striving for Justice: Accountability and the Crimes of the Khmer Rouge," a 1995 study for the U.S. Department of State. While there are obvious problems and complications associated with each option, they are not insurmountable given sufficient political will.

Peacebuilding in Cambodia: The Continuing Quest for Power and Legitimacy

Michael W. Doyle

Introduction

On July 5–6, 1997, Cambodia experienced a coup that erased most of the political gains made by United Nations Transitional Authority in Cambodia (UNTAC) in 1992–93. After an expenditure of more than $1.8 billion dollars for UNTAC, the death of 78 UNTAC soldiers and civilians (and many more Cambodians), and more than a billion dollars in foreign aid, Cambodia finds itself in the condition it was in 1990, before the UN peace operation began. Once again a government lacking legitimacy faces an internal insurgency on its border and isolation from the international community.

It was not supposed to turn out this way. The peace operation in Cambodia that culminated in the May 1993 elections was widely hailed as one of the UN's peacekeeping successes. But, as has become increasingly clear, what Cambodia also needed was peacebuilding—the institutional, social, and economic reforms that can serve to defuse or peacefully resolve conflict. Failure to build on a peace treaty can unravel a peacekeeping success. Only concerted

The author would especially like to thank Mallika Krishnamurthy for her research assistance; Benny Widyono, the secretary-general's representative in Cambodia (SGRC); Genevieve Merceur, of the SGRC staff; Ambassador Dato Deva Mohd. Ridzam and Din Merican of the Malaysian Embassy in Cambodia; more than 40 individuals interviewed in New York and Phnom Penh; and Suparidh Hy and the participants at an International Peace Academy seminar on Cambodian Peacebuilding on June 19, 1996. This chapter draws on *Peacebuilding in Cambodia*, from the IPA Peace Policy Briefing Series (New York: IPA, 1996).

action by the government, the donor community, NGOs, and the UN—both during and following UNTAC operations—could have kept peace on track and ensured a continued effort toward reconstruction, reconciliation, and a peaceful second set of national elections.

This chapter assesses how a peacekeeping operation that went relatively well turned into a peacebuilding experience that wasted the political opening it had created. It focuses on a gap between factions that had legitimacy without power and factions that had power without legitimacy. Some of the roots of the erosion lay in opportunities missed during the UNTAC period and in those neglected during the almost four years that followed the peace operation. The deeper roots of the crisis lay in the social, economic, and political structure of Cambodia and its unfortunate history the past 50 years.

From Coalition to Coup

During the four years preceding the July coup, Cambodia teetered on the edge between hope for a deepening peace and fear of escalating violence. For several years the uneasy coalition government headed by First Prime Minister Prince Ranarridh and Second Prime Minister Hun Sen held together, the urban economy experienced significant growth, and Cambodia looked forward to becoming a member of the Association of Southeast Asian Nations (ASEAN).

At the same time, however, Cambodia experienced little progress in building peace beyond that achieved by the 1991 Paris Peace Accords and the UNTAC peace process.[1] The country's fragile political and economic gains remained in constant jeopardy from the dangerous polarization within the government, the ongoing counter-insurgency war against the Khmer Rouge, and the sluggish revival of the rural economy. The CPP-FUNCINPEC rivalry created a bureaucratic and political stalemate. Partisan financial corruption seriously undermined the development process, and international drug trafficking was a growth industry. Illegal logging bled funds from the national budget into personal, party, and military coffers. At the same time, half of all government expenditures went to support the military. Millions of mines continued to litter the countryside and to maim and kill. All this in a country with an average per capita real income of about one-twentieth that of the

United States, an adult literacy rate of 38 percent, and a life expectancy of 52 years.

Starting with reports of an attempted coup in spring 1996, violent confrontations between CPP and FUNCINPEC forces marked the escalation of tensions. Constitutional procedures and effective government ground to a halt; neither the cabinet nor the National Assembly met. Essential legislation for Cambodia's planned entry into ASEAN and for the national election scheduled for May 1998 was stymied. On March 30, 1997, a grenade attack on a political rally of opposition leader Sam Rainsy produced 16 deaths and more than a hundred wounded. In May bodyguards for FUNCINPEC and the CPP battled in the streets, and on May 29, Hun Sen's bodyguards announced that the second prime minister had been the target of an assassination attempt. In June a pitched battle was fought in the streets of the capital and a rocket landed in the U.S. Embassy compound.

Four coup attempts were made between 1993 and 1997; the fifth, Hun Sen's of July 5–6, 1997, succeeded. (Previous attempts had been foiled when the parties united against dissidents or the two senior generals, Ke Kim Yan of the CPP and Nhek Bunh Chhay of FUNCINPEC, stopped them.) Given the weakness of the Cambodian state, the underdevelopment of the economy, and the "thinness" of Cambodian civil society, the coup should not have been a surprise.[2] But in retrospect, the timing of the July coup appears to have been triggered by two unpredicted events.

The first was the surprising breakup of the Khmer Rouge in 1996–97. In September 1996 Ieng Sary, foreign minister during the Pol Pot regime, defected with three "divisions" and control of the timber and gem-rich region around Pailin. After strenuous bargaining between Hun Sen and Ranariddh, Hun Sen won over Ieng Sary, whose cohorts then received a royal pardon and Pailin as a nearly independent fiefdom.

During the following summer reports of the capture of Pol Pot were hailed as a conclusion to Cambodia's era of troubles. In fact they were a sign of its escalation. The one thousand or so once-fearsome guerrillas holed up along the northwestern border finally turned on their founder in June 1997 when he summarily executed and then photographed vehicles crushing the bodies of his deputy, Son Sen and his family. In Cambodia, amidst genuine popular anticipation of long-delayed justice, the possibility of trial of Pol Pot's trial fanned the flames of CPP-FUNCINPEC discord. Handing him over became a bargaining chip for the amnesty of the remaining Khmer Rouge leaders, as Prince Ranariddh and Hun Sen competed for the allegiance of the Khmer Rouge. The Khmer Rouge offered disciplined cadres, effective guerrilla soldiers, and up to $200 million secreted in Southeast Asian bank accounts. As word of a deal between Khieu Samphan and Ranariddh began to circulate—a deal that would bring all the Khmer Rouge remnants over to FUNCINPEC—Hun Sen struck.

The other cause of the coup was the increasing competition and therefore the increased premium on allies fostered by the impending elections. The problem was not the elections per se,[3] which, as will be discussed below, were necessary to maintain legitimacy and establish a mutual connection between the Cambodian state and the people it ruled. The problem was the unraveling of the governing coalition. Tension escalated in 1996, when FUNCINPEC, alarmed that it had little influence in the administration of the countryside, demanded a share of the district-level offices. Control of the districts would be decisive in determining effective access to the voters. The CPP stalled in its response, and FUNCINPEC failed to provide a plausible, comprehensive list of candidates.

The underlying source of concern was that the winner of the elections would have the authority to rule alone (should he have won an absolute majority). This was a threat for the CPP, which according to an early 1997 public opinion poll was vastly unpopular: Only 20 percent questioned said they supported Hun Sen's party.[4] Yet the state officials who were members of Hun Sen's party had no other livelihood apart from their bureaucratic positions. Many had joined the Khmer Rouge in the early 1970s, fled to Vietnam in 1977 or 1978, and returned with the Vietnamese invasion in December 1978, holding government office since then. In addition rumors that King Sihanouk, the one political leader with wide rural legitimacy, might abdicate and run for election probably intensified Hun Sen's apprehension. For Ranariddh the prospect of an election became an opportunity to escape from the paper coalition that rendered FUNCINPEC powerless. He thus formed an electoral alliance with Sam Rainsy, who was widely popular among urban youth.

As tension mounted, Ranariddh began to arm his bodyguard

unit, allegedly with smuggled arms shipments, to match the much larger guard already surrounding Hun Sen. Hun Sen struck on July 5, 1997. Hundreds of FUNCINPEC supporters were rounded up, and at least 40, by the estimates of human rights groups, were summarily executed. As of early 1998 the former opposition was intimidated and civil society had run for cover. ASEAN membership is on hold at least until the 1998 elections. U.S., Australian, World Bank, (International Monetary Fund (IMF), and European Union (EU) aid to the government has been frozen. Tourism has ground to a halt. Private investors have instituted an informal freeze on new investments. Fifty thousand Cambodians are refugees on the Thai border. General Nhek Bun Chhay leads a military resistance in FUNCINPEC's name, and he has been joined by the few remnants of the Khmer Rouge. The new coalition (an unfortunate revival of the 1980s joint resistance to the CPP) operates uneasily on the Thai-Cambodian border.

The condition of Cambodia today confirms that the peacebuilding process was only begun when the parties signed the Paris Peace Accords in October 1991 and when UNTAC arrived in March 1992 to help implement it. Peacebuilding was stillborn, and the parties remained in a near state of war.

Roots of the Current Crisis
The roots of the current crisis lie in Cambodia's past and especially in victimization by its neighbors, in the underdevelopment of the Cambodian economy and polity, and in UNTAC's inability to jump-start the process of civic reform and economic rehabilitation.

Victimization
For much of its postwar history Cambodia has found itself in a dangerous neighborhood. Bombed by the United States during the Vietnam War, which radicalized intellectuals and peasantry, it fell prey to the Khmer Rouge in 1975, the worst fanatics in the second half of the twentieth century. Cambodia was rescued in 1978 but only by its historic enemy, Vietnam. It was then occupied by Vietnam for a decade.

As a result Cambodia has lacked the space in which to address the key challenges of modern development. It has faced crisis after crisis, and each before it had time to adjust to or resolve the previous one. Cambodia is now—at last—trying to recover from a combination of trials.

Cambodia is still seeking to overcome the legacies of colonialism. Indeed the first generation of postcolonial leadership is still in place. King Sihanouk was first enthroned by the French in 1941. Huge inequalities between urban and rural areas persist, typical of export-oriented, metropolitan-based, colonial economic development. Before these inequalities and dependencies were overcome, the 1978 Vietnamese invasion imposed a new kind of colonialism, as the People's Republic of Kampuchea (PRK) regime ruled from the "knapsack" of Vietnam in 1979, and Vietnam continued to govern until it withdrew its troops in from behind the scenes in 1989.[5] Prior to the Vietnamese withdrawal, the PRK renamed itself the State of Cambodia (SOC).

Cambodia is still recovering from the destruction inflicted by wars, beginning with the U.S. bombing and Khmer Rouge devastations and continuing into the civil wars of the 1990s. All left acute rehabilitation needs, not unlike those of countries such as Vietnam and Eritrea. Cambodia suffers from a postholocaust syndrome. The Khmer Rouge massacres left a desperate need for social reconstruction. Only a handful of monks, intellectuals, medical doctors, and trained lawyers survived these massacres. A massive deficit of social capital resulted, and many survivors carry deep psychological burdens that discourage reconstruction. Cambodia is a civil war survivor from the pitched battles of 1979–91 between government forces and the unified resistance on the Thai border. Like Mozambique and Angola, the reconciliation and reintegration of 370,000 refugees challenges the country's efforts to rebuild. Finally, like the economies of Eastern Europe, Cambodia is undergoing a postcommunist transition to a market economy begun by the SOC in 1991.

Any of these problems would constitute a serious challenge to a country as poor as Cambodia, which is unique in facing them all at once. Its efforts should be judged in light of this exceptional burden.

Underdevelopment and Dependence

Cambodia is fortunate in having a profound sense of nationhood and a revered national religion in Buddhism, but it lacks a capable modern state and integrated modern economy. The difficult, deep-rooted tasks of building a state and an economy remain. Services and industry, which tend to be concentrated in urban areas, account for 57 percent of GDP, but employ only 25 percent of the work force. The productive base must spread beyond cities. Unfortunately current trends suggest that these inequalities will worsen before they improve and Phnom Penh will be overwhelmed by job seekers. Cambodia's GDP grew at an average of 5.9 percent per year from 1990 to 1995. But while the urban and hotel sector grew at 20 percent per annum and construction at 15.2 percent, the rural economy stagnated as rice production grew at -.1 percent and livestock at 3.8 percent.[6] Expenditure patterns reveal similar disparities. Rural households have only 33 percent of the average household expenditure per day of Phnom Penh households and only 14 percent of the discretionary expenditure of their counterparts in Phnom Penh.[7]

Poverty and inequality both undermine the prospects for building peace. The large and growing gaps in income draw farmers into Phnom Penh and breed discontent and anger against the government. Discontent in turn undermines government incentives to democratize and increases the prospect of predatory human rights abuses. The gaps may also feed into possible support for the Khmer Rouge. Most important, income gaps waste the development potential of the vast bulk of the population.

Further complicating efforts to spur development and establish the rule of law is the weakness of the state. The Khmer Rouge destroyed the postcolonial state Cambodia inherited from the French and replaced it with a regime that abandoned all normal state functions and created a national prison camp. The Vietnamese kept effective sovereign authority in their own hands until 1989. However, the PRK did develop some capacity in the 1980s. It assisted in training officials, but only very small numbers. Anyone who was literate (and politically reliable) could be considered for a judgeship. Training in Eastern Europe often involved the rote learning of a weak technology—usually in Bulgarian or German. Many able individuals made the most of the Eastern Bloc training, but it was not that useful in coping with modern capitalist management and the dynamic development standards of contemporary East Asia. I met one official in his late 40s who had already learned Khmer, French, Vietnamese, and Bulgarian and was taking up English—all in the process of furthering his technical education. Nonetheless, despite the initiative and patience of officials such as this one, the Cambodian civil service is not ready to supervise modern economic development.

Hun Sen may enjoy unrivaled political control of Cambodia, but the state he heads is very weak. Budgetary dependence is significant: Almost one half of the total government budget (46 percent in 1995) was foreign financed.[8] Eighty-five percent of all public investment is foreign-financed, as is 18 percent of private investment. Between 1992 and 1994 aid commitments stagnated. Actual project aid and assistance commitments declined; but technical assistance (foreign experts) grew by 20–30 percent and direct assistance to the government budget grew from 0.5 to 27 percent.[9] Government salaries are clearly too low at $20 per month for the lower civil service and $1,000 per month for a minister. Income at those levels invites corruption and a consequent loss of national revenue. Illegal logging alone results in $100 million per annum in lost revenue when contracts do not go through the Ministry of Finance.

In light of the extensive destruction in Cambodia in the past 30 years, technical assistance is welcome, but current practices may prevent the building of capacity.

A vicious circle has been drawn around reform. Lacking an effective civil service, international donors cannot entrust projects to the Cambodian state. The World Bank and many bilateral donors tend to contract the implementation of their projects directly with international and some domestic NGOs.[10] Without experience, the state cannot develop capacity. Reforms required are difficult technically but even more so politically, since the civil service is appointed and is the major source of patronage as well as (with the army) security for the two parties. Broader measures of building trust are necessary, including, for example, the implementation of the Constitutional Council and free and fair elections. Short of these broader reforms, Cambodia will remain in a developmental crisis even if the July coup is reversed and the legitimacy of the government is restored.

UNTAC's Legacy
Some of Cambodia's current problems are the product of peacebuilding that did not take place during the UNTAC period.

UNTAC achieved many successes, but it also missed some significant opportunities to reform and assist the Cambodian state.

Although the Khmer Rouge rejected the peace process in midcourse, UNTAC successfully organized, for the first time in the UN's history, a nationwide election from the ground up. Over 90 percent of the electorate turned out to vote for peace, they said. The May 1993 election brought to power Cambodia's first elected government since the 1960s and placed Norodom Sihanouk on the throne as the reigning monarch of a new parliamentary democracy. But opposition from the Khmer Rouge and continuing distrust between the CPP and FUNCINPEC resulted in numerous acts of violence. Ongoing strife stymied efforts to canton and demobilize the factional armies and begin the rehabilitation of a society and economy devastated by the Vietnam War and four years of Khmer Rouge massacres. The national election had to be conducted amid continuing violence and intimidation.

UNTAC achieved significant successes in restoring key features of Cambodian civil society. It repatriated over 370,000 refugees, encouraged the formation of Cambodian NGOs, and engaged in human rights education. Most significantly, it gave Cambodian society a sense of participation in politics through the national election, and thereby helping to secure legitimacy for the state. But it failed to control the SOC civil service. In 1993 the successor to the SOC, the Royal Government of Cambodia (RGC), inherited the continuing war with the Khmer Rouge, still well armed and ready to fight. The RGC had to accommodate both the existing CPP-dominated civil service and add to its ranks the newly enrolled FUNCINPEC officials. The result was a bureaucratic stalemate in which the two parties blocked each other at the cost of overall government effectiveness.

UNTAC has been criticized for failing to demobilize both the armies and the CPP-controlled civil service. Former UNTAC officials reply that demobilizing the civil service was never in the UNTAC mandate and the SOC never agreed to it in the Paris Accords.[11] But it should be noted that UNTAC did not "control" the civil service, nor did it launch the rehabilitation (except in very minor ways) of the Cambodian economy, which it was supposed to do.[12]

Both the SOC and the Khmer Rouge undermined the Paris Accords—and each blamed the other. The SOC withheld its cooperation from UNTAC for the purpose of effecting control when the Khmer Rouge refused to demobilize. The Khmer Rouge refused to demobilize when UNTAC failed to neutralize the SOC. The wariness of each side appears to have been justified. But it also should be noted that while the Khmer Rouge denied UNTAC access to its zone, the SOC allowed UNTAC to deploy in its territory (85 percent of Cambodia).

Some observers have suggested that UNTAC control might have been more effective had it been combined with the training and building capacity of the SOC bureaucracy. Training would have transferred desired skills and might have provided the basis for cooperative control. Taken together this would have opened up the way for a more neutral, national public civil service. Senior former officials of UNTAC disagree, arguing that the parties would not have accepted so proactive a mandate at the Paris Peace negotiations. All can agree that a training function, if widely implemented, would have required an increase in the UNTAC budget. A mandate to modernize the bureaucracy was not out of the question in late spring 1993, but no one knew who would pay the factional armies in the period after the May election and before the formation of a sovereign government. (The UNTAC customs service experienced some success in this role as did the Australian police in Banteay Meanchey Province in 1993.) If UNTAC had combined control and training, it might then have handed over a more stable, responsive, and effective bureaucracy. But by May 1993 the UN was anxious to leave Cambodia in order to shift its focus to its increasing burdens in Somalia and Bosnia. An important lesson, then, that can be drawn from the UN peacekeeping effort in Cambodia is that peacekeeping will not lead to lasting peace without training for building peace.

Another shortcoming of UNTAC was its failure to jump start the rehabilitation of the Cambodian economy. The rehabilitation component of UNTAC, which was responsible for assessing needs, ensuring efficient and effective coordination of aid, and raising resources, was not fully operational until January 1993. It helped put a number of important financial and administrative reforms in place and averted several major crises, including hyperinflation, rice shortages, and government bankruptcy. Aid channeled through UNTAC did not, however, "benefit all areas of Cambodia, especially the disadvantaged, and reach all levels of society," as the

Declaration of Reconstruction required.[13] Aid flows during the UNTAC period, in fact, were biased in favor of urban areas, returnees, and relief in contrast to the declaration's call for developing rural areas and local capacity building. The urban bias artificially expanded the service sector (including prostitution), fostered high rates of consumer imports, and exacerbated income inequality.

In sum, the peace process in Cambodia left behind contradiction not reconciliation. It failed to resolve the fundamental problem that the competing factions lacked either legitimacy or power or both. The more powerful factions—the CPP's State of Cambodia and the Khmer Rouge—had committed cadres and effective military forces, but they lacked widespread public support and international recognition. Prince Ranariddh and FUNCINPEC had greater popularity and international support but a weak base of support in the bureaucracy and the military. The electoral defeat of Hun Sen and the CPP deprived them of legitimacy but did not wrest from them control of the bureaucracy and the army. The elections invested Ranariddh and FUNCINPEC with legitimacy but did not transfer genuine control of the state apparatus.

Restarting Peacebuilding

After the UNTAC period, Cambodia was left with a continuing war and an unreconciled political leadership and bureaucracy. The counter-insurgency war with the remaining 6,000 or so Khmer Rouge, holed up along the western border with Thailand, produced a thousand military and uncounted civilian casualties each year. Government forces pushed the Khmer Rouge guerrillas back into the jungles during the dry season, and each year guerrillas infiltrated back during the wet season. The war absorbed 40 percent or more of the government budget and led to more mines being laid in a country already having some of the world's highest rates of mine casualties. Government forces were not able to inflict decisive defeats on the guerrillas, and the guerrillas posed no military threat to the population centers. In 1996 and 1997 Khmer Rouge defections served to whet factional strife.

Meanwhile the state neglected the two keys to peacebuilding: improving the capacity of the civilian bureaucracy and bringing economic development to the countryside. While the capital, Phnom Penh, experienced a boom fueled by UN spending during the

UNTAC period, the rural areas experienced the added burden of inflation on top of the devastation of the previous 20 years. Urban-rural inequality continued to heighten, engendering rural anger with ominous overtones.

Long-term peacebuilding requires a coherent and dedicated government prepared to fulfill its commitments to develop an impartial judicial system and organize the crucial second national election, now scheduled for July 1998. Instead the CPP-FUNCIN-PEC rivalry created a bureaucratic stalemate, which compelled both parties to purge leading dissidents and reformers. Partisan financial corruption disrupted the development process.

The July 1997 coup rolled back much of the little progress that Cambodia had achieved since 1993. In response to the coup and continuing budget irregularities, the United States, Australia, the EU, the World Bank, and the IMF suspended all nonhumanitarian assistance. The UN General Assembly has refused to seat either the Hun Sen–Ung Huot delegation or the previous Ranariddh delegation. ASEAN has joined in a Friends of Cambodia group to mediate between the government and the opposition with a view to discovering ways to restore democratic legitimacy to the government now holding power in Phnom Penh; the peace-building deficit continues to impede Cambodian development.

All this raises two fundamental questions. First can peacebuilding be put back on track? And second should the international community bother to make a further investment in Cambodian peacebuilding? Cambodia has already received more than $1.8 billion for the UNTAC peace effort and $1.3 billion pledged in aid since then. Those who oppose further aid to Cambodia, argue that other countries are more deserving and more capable of using the aid effectively.

The international community should remain engaged in Cambodia for a number of reasons. Abandoning Cambodia will impact the vast majority of Cambodians who are still on the world's list of neediest individuals. Moreover the international community still has a stake in the success of one of its major peace operations. Cambodia's factions made commitments in the Paris Accords that the international community, represented by the UN, agreed to monitor and guarantee for the people of Cambodia. Cambodia's regional neighbors have an especially strong incentive to keep their neighborhood productive and secure. An unstable, crime-dominated

Cambodia would be very costly for Thailand, Laos, Vietnam, and Malaysia.[14] Lastly thousands of migrant Cambodians have risked their careers by returning home and entering government and business. Others have undertaken new and risky professions as human rights activists and journalists. Millions of Cambodians risked their lives to vote in May 1993. They should not and need not be abandoned.

Putting Peacebuilding Back on Track

Establishing domestic peace is a distinct and difficult task. Someone or something must be sovereign, guaranteeing law and order, by force if need be. Otherwise civil war simply continues. Victory by one side as in the July coup, partition among the contending factions, subordination to foreign rule, or national peacebuilding are the alternatives. In Cambodia only the last truly counts as a step toward long-term peace and development.

The challenges of building peace after the July coup are threefold. The first challenge is to restore legitimacy by establishing a new national coalition government and strengthening the rule of law and democratic participation. The second is to enhance the effectiveness of the state bureaucracy by reforming civilian and military institutions, thereby creating a national state capable of governing on a national rather than a partisan basis. In this way legitimacy and power can reinforce each other: The government will gain legitimacy, and the legitimate government will control the resources of a national impartial state. And, third, Cambodia needs to continue to develop a civil society as well as a market economy that reaches and benefits ordinary citizens, especially in the underdeveloped rural regions. All three must be met to put peacebuilding back on track. This will require international assistance and considerable good fortune.

Restoring Legitimacy. The first goal should be to restore an authentic governmental coalition of Hun Sen's, Ranariddh's, and Sam Rainsy's followers. Civil government in Cambodia has no alternative to a coalition. The coalition agreement should establish the broad outlines of government policies and define the sharing of ministries. This would give the Cambodian people and their leaders some time to restore a degree of political and economic stability. Without the restoration of a legitimate coalition there can be no one to organize credible elections, for no party can trust the others. Without the promise of a coalition continuing after the 1998 elections, neither the CPP or FUNCINPEC are likely to respect the electoral results. Moreover, administrative experience and legitimacy are scarce commodities in Cambodia—neither can be wasted.

One ideal but unlikely step toward a coalition would be a bilateral pardon from King Sihanouk, in which both Prince Ranariddh's alleged gun smuggling and Hun Sen's alleged direction of the 40 or more executions of senior FUNCINPEC officials both pardoned. The Ranariddh–Hun Sen government would resume as before. Implausible as this sounds, it should be remembered that the violence of the 1980s and of the 1993 election campaign did not preclude the shaky coalition of 1993–97. More realistic, perhaps, is a general pardon in which Ranariddh retires from politics and becomes king, and other FUNCINPEC-KNP leaders are reabsorbed into a government of national unity.

Broader measures of building trust also appear necessary, if only to help hold the coalition together. They include, for example, a greater role for the National Assembly and the implementation of the Constitutional Council. The National Assembly needs to play a more independent role in the legislative process. It needs to serve as a better watchdog over the government, a better provider for the constituencies, and a better representative of the diversity of the popular will. One good step could be taken with USAID's assistance—providing everything from desks and equipment to workshops on legislative procedures and duties—to the fledgling Cambodian legislature.

King Sihanouk could make the difference in two key confidence-building measures that could alleviate the tension between the political parties. The first would be to breathe life into the recently created Constitutional Council. At present, all Cambodia's laws are suspended between true legality and emergency dictat. Council membership should be chosen on a new, impartial, national basis, selected from all the political parties but encouraged to serve in an independent capacity (for example mandated to serve a fixed but staggered set of terms).

The RGC also should ensure that the National Election Commission is genuinely neutral and it should convene a group of eminent Cambodians from civil society and experts from the region and abroad to monitor the work of the Ministry of the Interior. Cambodia should seek the assistance of the UN (along with national and international NGOs) for technical support and as monitors of both the campaign and voting. Monitoring the election does little good if the voting is the conclusion of an oppressive and biased campaign environment. The World Bank Consultative Group could allocate and monitor aid for this purpose.

Creating a State That Works. A lesson for Cambodia is the importance of, on the one hand, a bureaucracy with the technical capabilities and political authority to make and implement governmental decisions and, on the other hand, increased reliance on open markets and transparent protection for contracts and private property.[15]

With regard to bureaucratic reform, the RGC must demonstrate its commitment to marketization in order to reduce the overall level of demand on public management and building capacity for the civil service. There is a broad consensus among Cambodian development experts on the need for a leaner and more effective state. Rapid economic development can be achieved in Cambodia with a smaller civil service, such as the one that led Thailand to economic growth beginning in the 1950s.[16] The Cambodian bureaucracy should eventually shed tens of thousands of officials in the civil service and equivalent numbers in the military, while enhancing capabilities all around. An effective state should play a key role in developing the rule of law by ensuring the state police and judiciary have the means to implement the law impartially.

Incentives for military predation can be reduced only by military demobilization and improving the training and logistics of the remaining forces. But demobilization is costly in the short run. If it is attempted without a comprehensive plan to resettle and retrain soldiers, they are likely to turn into marauders. In Uganda one careful study found that dismissed soldiers were 100 times more likely to commit crimes than those with land or other assistance.[17]

The government also should introduce transparency in all contracts. The Cambodia Development Council should make all its investment contracts and concessions public, and the government should publish all private and public investment and aid contracts. Cambodia faces no external threats sufficiently serious to justify secrecy. Nor does secrecy allow Cambodia to exercise monopoly bargaining power to improve its contract terms. Secrecy today serves merely to cover corruption. Transparency works to the advantage of all reformers and may, indeed, enhance Cambodia's bargaining power by limiting the ability of foreign investors to play Cambodian officials and ministries against each other. Donors can require that all foreign assistance projects be made public. The IMF set the standard in 1996 when it sanctioned the RGC for a failure of transparency in the sale of state assets.

Developing a Civil Society and Market Economy. Civil socialization works by reducing demands on the managerial capacity of the state and improving a society's capacity to articulate and meet public needs. It also generates employment and careers outside the bureaucracy and the army. UNTAC helped open a space for hundreds of new, indigenous Cambodian NGOs. In step with the moderating of civil war, traditional Buddhist organizations began to reestablish their role as spiritual guides and community organizers in the rural areas.

Marketization has created new sources of livelihood in Cambodia's cities and towns. International donors' requirement of transparent investment contracts can limit corruption and encourage broad-based economic development that takes advantage of Cambodia's low wages and access to ASEAN and other international markets. Apparel and other light manufacturing are currently experiencing a boom around the cities. Well-meaning foreign activists are protesting child labor. A better focus would be establishing the right to unionize and promoting basic health and safety standards. Working in a clean, safe factory near their parents is a step up for the many Cambodian children who toil on the rice farms and for the unfortunate thousands who work in the brothel villages that surround Phnom Penh.

The UNDP has developed the single most promising model for combined market and democratic development in the countryside. The Cambodia Area Rehabilitation and Regeneration (CARERE) Project II, or "Seila" (which means "foundation stone" in Khmer), combines rural infrastructure development, local participatory decision making, and state capacity building. Designed as a pilot for five provinces, Seila establishes a chain of elected committees beginning with the village development committee, which elects a commune committee, which in turn elects district and then provincial development committees. The provinces are given independent budgets (as are the districts) to allocate among worthy projects proposed by the villages and communes. This is designed to be bottom-up, not top-down, democratization. It embodies the potential of building participatory, local self-determination and accountability. The UNDP assists the provincial committee with technical advice designed to build planning capacity and responsible budgetary control at the provincial level. Seila won the support of the national government and five provincial governors. It was scheduled to go into expanded operation in 50 villages.[18] The autocratic structure of the Cambodian village will not be changed overnight, but even first steps toward consultation and accountability, when connected to real investments, can begin to mobilize rural efforts.

International Facilitation

Outsiders are needed; they control the international legitimacy, the capital, and the markets that the CPP needs. In September 1997 the five permanent members of the UN Security Council and ASEAN wisely combined forces to focus diplomatic efforts. The result was ASEAN's decision to postpone Cambodia's membership and the UN's decision not to seat the coup delegation. Such diplomacy sends a clear signal of the international and regional interest in the continued progress of peace in Cambodia.

An UNTAC II is out of the question (no one in the international community is prepared to invest the manpower or money), but something more than the monitoring of a future election is required. Monitoring will be too late to correct abuses or assist the coalition. Cambodia needs a UN Peace-building Mission for Cambodia (UNPMC) that will assist in the planning for a national election as well as in building the capacity of the civilian and military bureaucracy. Intensive monitoring and technical help worked in El Salvador in 1994 to train a national civilian police, begin the reform of the judiciary, and produce a poll that allowed the beleaguered FMLN former-guerrilla movement to gain a toehold in the government.[19] It should work in Cambodia as well, where the voters have a standard exemplified in the free UNTAC elections of 1993. NGOs need to add intensive campaigns of voter education, modeled on the successful ones organized by UNTAC, especially in the regions the Khmer Rouge barred from UN access in 1993. UNPMC should monitor and provide technical assistance only. Cambodians should organize the elections to develop indigenous democratic capacity if for no other reason.

Investing in the long-run development of human rights and a vibrant civil society also calls for a continuation of the UN Center for Human Rights. UNCHR assists the government in a variety of ways, including human rights education and training, but it is urgent that it retain its active and outspoken reporting of abuses. The center's rigorous monitoring is a valuable source of information. Without the cover that UNCHR provides, local human rights activists believe that they would be forced into silence.

The international community should be prepared to restore all aid to a Cambodian government that agrees to a UNPMC. The current cuts in foreign aid and the collapse of international private investment are powerful incentives for resuming the path of comprehensive peacebuilding. Should the government refuse a UNPMC, aid should be limited only to assistance that directly serves to support the poor and builds indigenous nongovernmental organizations and a civil society free of government control. If the government tries to exploit or tax the aid, it should cease.

Finally ASEAN has a key role to play. Having been a pawn of global politics and invasion, Cambodia is eager to obtain the status of a full member of the region by joining ASEAN, which has a stake in Cambodia's success. Cambodia will provide a vibrant market for ASEAN products and a place for investment with access to trade preferences for countries such as Singapore and later Malaysia and Thailand as they graduate from that status. Failure in Cambodia, on the other hand, will generate spillover military strife, drug cartels, and regional contests for subversive influence.

Conclusion

It is time for King Sihanouk's last hurrah. The man who led Cambodia to independence from France in 1955, maintained the precarious balance between the North Vietnamese and the United States in the 1960s, and orchestrated the Paris Peace Accords of 1991, again needs to lead Cambodia in a peace-building campaign to restore legitimacy and effectiveness to the Cambodian state. Though ill and frail, he alone can mobilize a national coalition of all the parties and call on the international community to once again take on an active peace-building role.

Peacebuilding in Cambodia tests whether the antagonists of the civil wars can be turned into the protagonists of party politics. The Paris Peace Accords were comprehensively negotiated among the factions over 10 years and received the full support of the international community, together with the deployment of 23,000 peacekeepers in 1992–93 and an expenditure of about $4 billion in peacekeeping and foreign aid. Smaller efforts in less divided countries have worked, for example in Namibia, El Salvador, and Mozambique. Will this larger, more difficult test be passed? If not, what are the prospects for peacebuilding where the divisions are even more severe and have an ethnic or religious basis, as in Bosnia or Angola?

Notes

1. See U.S. General Accounting Office, *Cambodia: Limited Progress on Free Elections, Human Rights, and Mine Clearing* (Washington, DC: GAO, 1996).

2. In December 1996 a near consensus existed among Cambodia experts that the chances of a coup in the near future were about 50-50.

3. For a criticism of electoral strategies for peace, see Jack Snyder and Karen Ballentine, "Nationalism and the Marketplace of Ideas," *International Security*, Vol. 21, no. 2, pp. 5–40.

4. Keith Richburg and R. Jeffrey Smith, "Cambodian Chaos," *International Herald Tribune*, July 14, 1997, p. 4.

5. For a thoughtful discussion of Cambodia's political legacy, see Aun Porn Moniroth, *Democracy in Cambodia: Theories and Realities*, trans. Khieu Mealy (Phnom Penh: Cambodian Institute for Cooperation and Peace, 1995). For background on these issues, see Ben Kiernan and Chantou Boua, eds., *Peasants and Politics in Kampuchea 1942–1981* (London: Zed Press, 1982); Michael Vickery, *Kampuchea: Politics, Economics, and Society* (Boulder, CO: Lynne Rienner, 1986); and David Chandler, "Three Visions of Politics in Cambodia," in *Keeping the Peace: Multidimensional UN Operations in Cambodia and El Salvador*, ed. Doyle et al. (Cambridge University Press, 1997).

6. Royal Government of Cambodia, *First Socioeconomic Development Plan, 1996–2000*, p. 85.

7. Ibid., Table 2.3, p. 17.

8. Ibid., p. 90.

9. John P. McAndrew, *Aid Infusions, Aid Illusions,* Working Paper No. 2 (Phnom Penh: Cambodian Development Resource Institute, January 1996).

10. "Recommendation to the International Committee on the Rehabilitation and Reconstruction of Cambodia, 1995" in *Cambodia Rehabilitation Program: Implementation and Outlook: A World Bank Report for the 1995 ICORC Conference* (Washington, DC: World Bank, 1995). Also see Benny Widyono, "Reconstruction of the Post-Conflict Public Administrative Machinery in Cambodia" (prepared for the Interregional Seminar "On Restoring Government Administrative Machinery in Situations of Conflict," March 13–15, 1996, Rome), and Royal Government of Cambodia, "The Administrative Reform: An Overview" (prepared for the Donor's Meeting, Phnom Penh, May 10, 1996).

11. UNTAC's mandate specifically charge it to exercise supervision over "agencies, bodies, and other offices [which] could continue to operate in order to ensure normal day-to-day life." For background on the new features of the UN mandate in Cambodia see Steven Ratner, *The New UN Peacekeeping* (New York: St. Martin's, 1995); Trevor Findlay, *The UN in Cambodia* (Stockholm: SIPRI, 1995); Janet Heininger, *Peacekeeping in Transition: The United Nations in Cambodia* (New York: Twentieth Century Fund, 1994); and Nishkala Suntharalingam, "The Cambodian Settlement Agreements," in *Keeping the Peace: Multidimensional UN Operations in Cambodia and El Salvador,* ed. Michael Doyle et al. (New York: Cambridge University Press, 1997).

12. On the control function, see Article 6 of the "Agreement on a Comprehensive Political Settlement of the Cambodia Conflict" and UNTAC Mandate Annex 1, Section B; New York: United Nations, October 30, 1991.

13. See Elizabeth Uphoff, "Quick Impacts, Slow Rehabilitation in Cambodia," in *Keeping the Peace,* ed. Doyle et al. (New York: Cambridge University Press, 1997), pp. 186–205.

14. The press has been suggesting a connection between the July coup and Teng Bunma, who is said to have bankrolled it and to be personally involved, according to U.S. officials, in the transshipment of drugs in Southeast Asia. Teng Bunma recently received a timber concession of one million acres. "Cambodian Tycoon Acquires Major Timber Concession," Reuters, October 2, 1997.

15. The general case for marketization is made in World Bank, *From Plan to Market: World Development Report 1996* (Washington, DC: World Bank, 1996). See also Mancur Olson, "Disorder, Cooperation, and Development:

A Way of Thinking About Cambodian Development" (Phnom Penh: Cambodian Institute for Cooperation Peace, 1996).

16. Robert J. Muscat, "Rebuilding Cambodia: Problems of Governance and Human Resources," in *Rebuilding Cambodia: Human Resources, Human Rights, and Law,* ed. Fred Brown (Washington, DC: Foreign Policy Institute, 1993), pp. 13–42.

17. J. P. Azam, *Some Economic Consequences of the Transition from Civil War to Peace* (Washington, DC: World Bank, 1994).

18. United Nations Development Program and Royal Government of Cambodia, Project Document CMB/95/011/01/31, CARERE II (Phnom Penh: February 1996), and interviews with Scott Leiper, UNDP, May 1996. For background, see RGC, UNDP, and UN Office for Project Services, *Building the Foundation of the Seila Programme: The 1996 Work Plan of the Cambodia Area Rehabilitation and Regeneration Project* (Phnom Penh: March 1996).

19. Ian Johnstone, *Rights and Reconciliation* (Boulder, CO: Lynne Rienner, 1995).

The Challenge of Sustainable Economic Growth and Development in Cambodia

Naranhkiri Tith

Introduction

Since 1970 Cambodia has been through major changes in its economic, political, and social systems. From 1970 to 1991, the Cambodian people suffered a great deal as a result of civil strife, foreign occupation, and massive man-made errors in economic and social management. The country lost an estimated two million people or 25 percent of its population as a result of the genocidal policy of the Khmer Rouge and foreign invasion. Most of its infrastructure was destroyed, and its small endowment of human capital was decimated or forced to flee the country. The standard of living of the average Cambodian as measured by per capita GDP was $260 in 1995, and the nation was ranked by the World Bank as among the 20 poorest in the world. Cambodian per capita income in 1995 represented only two thirds of the 1969 level.

From 1975 until 1991, the Cambodian economy operated under a centrally planned system. Cambodia was integrated into the economic and trading system of the Eastern bloc or the Council for Mutual Economic Assistance (CMEA). For this reason Cambodia was practically cut off from the world's market economies.

Some modest systemic reform was introduced by the People's Republic government in 1985 and accelerated in 1989, reflecting changes in the communist system in Europe. However, only with the arrival of the UNTAC in 1992 was Cambodia able to fully reconnect with the world economy. This led to relatively large inflows of private and official financial and technical resources. This relatively large influx of resources allowed the Cambodian economy to record relatively high growth rates combined with low inflation. However, this phenomenon also caused Cambodia to become highly dependent on foreign humanitarian, technical, and financial assistance for its survival.

Thus today Cambodia must not only make the transition from a centrally planned economic system to a market-oriented one, it must also make the transition from a war economy to a peace economy, and from a poor and underdeveloped economy to a more prosperous and developed one. It is indeed a formidable task for Cambodia's leaders and its people, as well as for the international community involved in helping the country to rebuild its shattered society and economy.

This chapter describes the economic challenges facing Cambodia and assesses the effectiveness of the policies adopted to reform the economy and promote economic growth. In the case of Cambodia, where the structure and level of population, income, and production are not well balanced, macroeconomic variables such as GDP growth rates and inflation rates alone may not be appropriate or sufficient for measuring the success or failure of economic management and performance in the long run. Other factors, such as structural change, income distribution, poverty levels, education and health services, environmental issues, unemployment, and underemployment, are also crucial to the evaluation of the impact of the reform program on Cambodian society. The true measure of success in transition for Cambodia, as professor James Riedel has suggested, is whether the combination of high rates of growth and low inflation is sustained over a period of two to four decades. Only then can Cambodia escape the cycle of poverty and political and social instability.

Key Developmental Constraints and Challenges
This section provides a brief survey of Cambodia's key developmental constraints and challenges, namely its resource endowment and the legacy of the centrally planned economic system.[1]

Human Resource Development
Cambodia has a population of about 10.2 million (1995), growing at an estimated rate of 2.5 to 2.8 percent per year.[2] About 85 percent of the population lives in rural areas and depends on farming as well

as nonfarming income for its living. Regionally the population is largely concentrated (60 percent) in six provinces located in the central plains and around the capital, Phnom Penh. The average population density of around 50 persons per square kilometer is relatively low compared to neighboring countries, such as Thailand (108) and Vietnam (195). However, it varies widely among provinces ranging from 4 in the northeastern provinces to 160 in the central provinces around Phnom Penh.

As a result of the war the Cambodian population is young (at least half are under 18 years), and, women constitute the majority (52.6 percent) of adults. Life expectancy is around 52 years, an improvement from the low of around 40 years during the Khmer Rouge period. Estimates of literacy vary widely from a recent figure of 85 percent provided by the government to only 65 percent according to the World Bank. There are signs that the majority of the population is physically weakened by malnutrition and traumatized by prolonged mental and physical hardship resulting from years of warfare and civil strife. Malnutrition was estimated at around 10 percent (1992) in Phnom Penh and 20 percent in the provinces.

One of the most tragic consequences of nearly two decades of social and economic dislocation and destruction is the emergence of extremely "vulnerable" groups within the Cambodian population. Prominent among these groups are female heads of households, refugees returning from the Thai border camps, and internally displaced persons. Finally there are about 350,000 handicapped. This number continues to climb as there are still about nine million unexploded land mines buried throughout the country. Cambodia has the distinction of having the highest number of amputees per capita in the world. The vulnerable groups are among the poorest in Cambodia and require special attention from the government and NGOs. In addition there is a pervasive health problem in the country, especially in rural areas where access to health care services, safe water, and adequate sanitation is still very limited.

After four years of Khmer Rouge rule (1975–79), Cambodia's education system was totally destroyed. During this period a large number of the country's estimated 20,000 teachers, other educational personnel, and technicians and professionals either died or left the country. Many schools and books as well as other educational equipment were destroyed. It is estimated that one in four of the adult population was illiterate at the end of 1979. During the 1980s the education system recovered substantially, but its quality remains poor, especially in the vocational, technical, and scientific fields. Poor education and other constraints in human resources will have a detrimental impact on labor productivity and weaken Cambodia's ability to adopt a strategy of export-led industrialization based on skilled and semiskilled labor.

Sustainable Natural Resource Use

Cambodia is relatively well endowed with natural resources, including minerals as well as timber, inland and coastal fisheries, and various agro-ecological conditions suited to a wide range of crops and livestock. The country is also well served by one of the most important rivers in Asia, the Mekong, with great potential for irrigation and generation of hydroelectricity.

Agriculture. Agriculture, animal husbandry, fishing, and forestry contribute almost 45 percent to GDP. Thirty percent of GDP originates from the rice and rubber sectors alone. Rice is by far the most important crop in Cambodia. Because of low soil fertility and the limited use of fertilizer, rice yields in Cambodia are the lowest in Asia, averaging 1.3 tons/ha, compared to 2.2 tons/ha, 3.5 tons/ha, and 4.3 tons/ha for Thailand, Vietnam, and Indonesia, respectively. This leaves room for higher yields through the use of multiple cropping, mechanization, and fertilizer. Rubber used to be the second most important foreign exchange earner for the country. Now, most rubber trees are old and need replanting to increase productivity. The potential for rubber production remains good for Cambodia, especially in production by small plantation holders.

Forestry. In the early 1970s Cambodia had a large forested area by Asian standards, with nearly 70 percent of its land area still under forest cover. However, Cambodia's forest area has been reduced to a mere 35 percent as a result of rapacious and uncontrolled logging. Global Witness, a British environmental NGO, has warned that:

> mismanagement and corruption within the RGC is now responsible for the destruction of Cambodia's forests on a scale that dwarfs all activity in the years prior to 1995. Environment degra-

dation caused by the destruction of Cambodia's forest has a direct and adverse effect on almost every aspect of human activity in Cambodia.[3]

Fisheries. Because of unique ecological conditions, mainly the annual flooding of the Great Lake (Tonle Sap), freshwater fish are abundant. Offshore areas also have abundant fish. As one of the most valuable resources of Cambodia, the Tonle Sap ecology must be carefully protected. However, this valuable natural asset has been deteriorating since the 1950s, and decline has accelerated since 1975. The main causes appear to be closely linked to environmental deterioration, including increased siltation and destruction of substantial portions of flooded forest resulting in the reduction of fish nursery and feeding areas. Overfishing and illegal fishing may also be significant causes of the decline in fish yield.[4]

Traditionally Cambodians have not engaged in fishing activities, and commercial fishing is not yet well developed owing to a lack of skill and capital. However, the potential benefit from marine fishing, shrimp farming, and aquaculture is as good as in neighboring countries and could be a good source of extra income for farmers, provided that environmental safeguards to farmers are strictly enforced.

Minerals. There is little mineral resource exploitation in Cambodia. Besides gems and phosphate, which are now being mined, there are indications that some deposits of bauxite, gold, phosphate, and limestone warrant further exploration. Other potential mineral deposits that may be commercially promising include iron ore, manganese, tin, copper, lead, zinc, and cilia. After a break of 20 years, the government reopened offshore oil and gas exploration in 1991, and bids were called in early 1992 for onshore exploration. Territorial disputes between Thailand and Vietnam prevented explorations for oil and gas from expanding further.

Only with a thorough geological mapping can the commercial viability of these mineral resources be known with a sufficient degree of certainty. For the moment such mapping is taking place only in the gas and oil subsector where some serious exploration activities are being undertaken. Even in this field only limited exploration is being done onshore. Almost all explorations are being carried out offshore.

Industry and Tourism

Accounting for about 20 percent of GDP, Cambodia's industrial sector is small but relatively diversified. It includes mining, manufacturing, construction, and public utilities. In the long run the manufacturing sector is the most important source for generating employment and income as well as foreign exchange earnings. To enhance the manufacturing sector, the government must design and executed a comprehensive plan for the industrialization of Cambodia. This plan must be export-oriented and executed primarily by the private sector with the government playing a supporting role. It also must be labor-intensive at first and become skill- or technology-intensive at a later stage. For this to happen, the government will need to reform and upgrade the education system. Infrastructure must be upgraded and updated, and trade and payments systems must be open.

The potential for a responsible tourism industry is very promising and could attract important foreign investment as well as create a great number of jobs for low-and semiskilled Cambodian workers. Cambodia's cultural and artistic heritage is rich and diversified, as can be seen in the Angkor Wat complex and the variety of folklore. Cambodia's pristine beaches and crystal-clear water along the Gulf of Thailand are still unspoiled by mass tourism. These relatively untouched cultural and natural sites can be responsibly transformed into a major source of foreign exchange earnings.

The Past as Prologue: The Legacy of Communism

A better understanding of recent economic and political developments in Cambodia requires a brief survey of the major events of the past two decades.

Democratic Kampuchea Period: Social Engineering Madness

Immediately after Phnom Penh fell to the Khmer Rouge in 1975, the government of Democratic Kampuchea (DK) was established with Pol Pot, the victorious guerrilla leader, as prime minister. The DK government launched a radical social engineering experiment in communal and social organization. Proclaiming its intention of totally breaking with the past and ready to use any means necessary, including mass killing to ensure the success of its policies, DK leadership set out to transform Cambodian society and economy into an agrarian "utopia."

The Khmer Rouge government started this drastic social and

economic transformation by abolishing and outlawing all private property. Deliberately, most industrial enterprises and infrastructure were neglected, money was banned, and foreign contacts, including trade, were forbidden. Inhabitants were evicted from the cities and were forced to work under inhuman conditions in gigantic rural irrigation projects later known as "Pol Pot's canals." Workers were paid in food rations and required to surrender all production to central control. Anyone showing signs of resistance or doubt was swiftly and severely punished, including by death.

The Khmer Rouge system was based on the collectivization of the agricultural sector. Planning to turn Cambodia into a vast rice field, the Khmer Rouge were obsessed with the idea of making Cambodia agriculturally self-sufficient and convinced that the solution resided in building a vast network of irrigation canals similar to the one that existed in the Angkor period. Village cooperatives were established as the basic blocks of the system. In turn these cooperatives were consolidated into large communes.

The devastating economic effects of this radical and inhuman regime were to change Cambodian society beyond recognition. As Milton Osborne, an Australian historian soberly observed:

> Phnom Penh was forcibly evacuated; existing patterns of Cambodian society with roots stretching back more than a thousand years were ended at one stroke; the Buddhist church ceased to exist; money as a means of exchange was eliminated; and we know that the population labored long hours in the fields working toward agricultural self-sufficiency and a new program of irrigation. But we will never know just how many Cambodians were killed.[5]

The human and economic costs were monumental. Children were separated from their parents. Malnutrition, disease, and summary executions were widespread. An estimated two million people—25 percent of the population—died or were killed. The extent of the damage to the Cambodian economy in just four years of under the Khmer Rouge regime was captured by the IMF:

> When the People's Republic of Kampuchea was established in January 1979, there was no private property, and property claims

that existed before 1975 had been dispersed or destroyed. The virtual disappearance of the educated elite meant that administrators had to be selected from people with little prior experience. Industry and agriculture had been devastated. There were no functioning schools or medical facilities and virtually no medical supplies.[6]

Khmer People's Republic Period: Beginning of Rehabilitation

The Vietnamese invasion of Cambodia in December 1978 dealt a mortal blow to the DK regime. In 1979 the country was renamed the People's Republic of Kampuchea (PRK) and more orthodox centrally planned economic system was introduced by the Vietnamese-installed government of Pen Sovann and Heng Samrin. From 1980, the focus was on rehabilitating and reconstructing the economy and society, including the drafting of a new criminal law and civil code, the repair and building of infrastructure, the stimulation of agricultural and industrial production, and, later, the encouragement of the private sector. The people were allowed to return to their original communities, including the cities. However, many rural residents chose not to stay in rural areas. Instead they moved into the cities and occupied property that had been abandoned. Among the most important economic decisions of the new regime were the reactivation of the Central Bank and the introduction of a new currency, the riel, in March 1980. The main foreign economic and financial assistance came from the former CMEA bloc.

Despite these changes, the new government's emphasis remained on reorganizing Cambodia into a classic command economy. The PRK first attempted to implement a modified form of collectivized agriculture, based on administrative and political units of people's revolutionary committees known as Krom Samaki. These committees were set up at all administrative levels, starting from the district level to the provincial level, as well as among professional groups, such as trade unions or women's associations.

The PRK government was not able to implement the collectivization of the economy as envisaged, partly because of the major changes that occurred in the socialist countries in Europe and Vietnam in the mid-1980s, as well as from the lack of administrative capability. This failure was recognized by the PRK's leadership at the Fifth Party Congress in 1986. There the private sector was formally recognized as one of the five official sectors in the economy; the others included the state, the collective, the joint venture, and the family sectors. The economy was opened up to foreign direct investment through joint ventures.

During 1986–88 additional reform measures were introduced. These included the restoration of private use (but not ownership) of land to boost agricultural production; the granting of greater autonomy to provincial authorities and managers of state enterprises; the delayed introduction of a tax system; and the freedom for family, private, and joint ventures to function alongside the state and collective economies. With these reforms in place, the Cambodian economy was gradually recovering in all sectors, albeit rising from a very low base. With the return of farmers to their original communities, crop production, especially rice production, started to increase modestly. Similarly, as the cities started to be populated again, industrial production resumed with imported inputs and machinery financed with credit from the Eastern Bloc countries. In return exported agricultural products were used to pay for part of those imports from the CMEA countries. At the same time border trade with neighboring countries, especially Thailand and Vietnam, began to flourish.

Beginning in 1989 the pace of reform accelerated and the scope expanded. A number of important new laws were approved by the legislative body. They included the lifting of price controls with the exception of some key commodities, such as petroleum, electricity, cement, iron, and fertilizer; the restoration of private ownership, including the right to inherit property and build on private land; a decree on foreign investment designed to encourage joint venture state-owned enterprises (SOEs); the privatization of SOEs through leasing or outright sale; and autonomy to most SOEs.

It appeared that policy reforms were starting to have considerable impact on the economy, especially in Phnom Penh where a modern hotel, the Cambodiana, was completed and a number of banks were opened. More than 12,000 private establishments, including more than 1,500 medium-sized units were reported to be operating in the capital city. In addition the supply of consumer durables as well as that of luxury consumer goods increased. These goods came mostly through border trade.

The Paris Agreements and the UNTAC Interregnum

The Declaration on the Rehabilitation and Reconstruction of Cambodia of the 1991 Paris Peace Accords provided a new framework for the reconstruction of Cambodia. It also made it possible for the Cambodian government to appeal to official donors, international and regional financial organizations, the UN, and NGOs for contributions. The declaration called for an initial and immediate focus on the provision of food, security, health care, housing, education and training, and transportation as well as the restoration of Cambodia's existing infrastructure and public utilities. The implementation of a long-term plan for Cambodia's reconstruction and development would await the formation of a government following the elections and the determination and adoption of its policies. However, the declaration stipulated that the reconstruction phase should promote Cambodian entrepreneurship and make use of the private sector, among others, to help advance sustainable growth. It also stipulated that following the formation of a new government, Cambodia's international donors would create a consultative group, the International Committee on the Reconstruction of Cambodia (ICORC), in order to "harmonize and monitor the contribution that will be made by the international community to the reconstruction of Cambodia."[7]

Within this framework the first ministerial meeting on the rehabilitation and reconstruction of Cambodia that took place in Tokyo in June 1992 pledged $880 million for the rehabilitation and reconstruction of Cambodia. At the Tokyo meeting the ICORC was formally established. Chaired by Japan, the ICORC convenes annually, with the venue normally alternating between Paris and Tokyo.

Thus the Paris Peace Accords not only provided a chance for Cambodia to regain its sovereignty, they also provided a framework and a commitment from the international community to provide long-term financial and technical assistance to help Cambodia rehabilitate and reconstruct its shattered economy and society. After 1991 the Cambodian economy was further enhanced by the increase in the demand for goods and services from some 20,000 UNTAC personnel involved in maintaining the peace and administering elections.

Unfortunately UNTAC's massive presence in Cambodia also had its bad side. According to William Shawcross:

the continuing arrival of UNTAC troops and civil administrators had an enormous impact on Cambodia's economy, especially Phnom Penh. UNTAC's international officials were paid a per diem of $145, while the average annual income in Cambodia was approximately $160. Land value, rents, and the prices of services and utilities soared, with no commensurate increase in government wages. As a result a double economy quickly developed and a large proportion of civil servants left their desks in order to profit from the private sector boom. In Phnom Penh inflation, corruption, and nepotism became ever more pervasive. New brothels were established and AIDS began to spread.[8]

There were also other major social and economic problems generated by the transition from a centrally planned system to a market-oriented one. These problems included the acceleration of inflation, the worsening of income distribution, the lack of linkages between development in the cities and the rural areas, and the increase in unemployment, insecurity, lawlessness, and corruption. In addition the balance of payments and debt problems also worsened.

An Assessment of Recent Economic Performance (1993–96)

With the newly elected government installed, a program for reconstruction and sustainable growth was introduced at the end of 1993. The main macroeconomic objectives of the 1994–96 structural adjustment and stabilization program were maintaining real growth of 7 to 8 percent per year; reducing the inflation rate to a rate comparable with partner countries or 5 percent by 1995; strengthening worldwide position by reducing the current account deficit to 9 percent of GDP by 1996, and raising international reserves.

Accomplishments

By any standard one cannot help but be impressed by the recent economic performance of Cambodia. From Table 1, we can observe that during the 1991–96 period real GDP grew at an average of 6.1 percent per year, albeit from a very low base. The exchange rate has remained fairly stable despite the shaky and precarious situation in the fiscal and monetary sectors. Thanks to the United States granting Most Favored Nation Status to Cambodia and the Generalized System of Preferences granted by some European countries, export growth has accelerated, especially in the recently established textile industry. Prior to mid-1997 there was a boom in construction and tourism—two labor intensive sectors—and are important sources of employment in a country where unemployment and underemployment are still extremely high and widespread.

The service sector has been the most dynamic and is geared toward the trade, hotel, and catering services. The service sector has been buoyed mainly by the impressive increase in the number of tourists visiting Cambodia, which increased from 5,000 a month in 1991 to about 15,000 in 1996. Responding to the surge in tourism, a number of well-known international luxury hotel chains, such as the Japanese Intercontinental group, the Singaporean Raffles group, and the French Sofitel group, have rushed to build large complexes in Phnom Penh and Siem Reap, a city near the famous ruins of Angkor.

Cambodia also has been successful in fighting inflation. That it was able to lower its inflation rate from triple to single digits in a short period, despite the presence of major financial and fiscal difficulties and major institutional weaknesses is indeed impressive. This success was based on two important factors: the availability of foreign assistance, such as budget support, and the ability of major international financial institutions such as the IMF and the World Bank, to design reform measures and monitor very closely their implementation.

Cambodia's recent macroeconomic performance looks even more impressive when compared with other former centrally planned economies in transition in Europe. Practically all former socialist countries, especially those in Eastern Europe and the former Soviet Union, experienced sharp and protracted output and trade collapse combined with hyperinflation during the early period of systemic reform. Cambodia along with other Asian economies in transition, such as China, Laos, and Vietnam, have recorded high and positive real growth rates. The balance of payment and budget deficits became more manageable thanks to external financial inflows. (See Table 1.)

The IMF has identified a number of exogenous and structural factors that allowed the three Asian countries in transition to avoid output collapse and hyperinflation. The most important are:

- In contrast to countries in transition in Eastern Europe and the Former Soviet Union, the three Southeast Asian countries had larger and more family-based agriculture with a labor surplus. Except for China, they also had relatively small state-owned industrial sectors. For instance Cambodia had less than 200 state enterprises, and Vietnam had about 12,000 compared with hundreds of thousands in such countries as Russia and Poland.

- The Asian countries in transition were less integrated with the CMEA bloc in terms of production, trade, and aid. Therefore, the impact of the CMEA collapse in 1991 was not as harmful as in the European countries in transition.

- The proximity of the Asian countries in transition to other Asian economic powerhouses creates a dynamic network of trade and investment among these countries, which, in turn, is conducive to high growth. For instance the major share of foreign direct investment in the Asian countries in transition originated from ASEAN, Korea, and Taiwan.

- Owing to the relatively short period of central economic planning in these Asian countries, the market legacy remained sufficiently strong to allow quick and positive responses to the reform process, once the state's constraints were removed.

A closer look at the recent economic performance of Cambodia, however, reveals a number of important weaknesses. When the rate of real growth is adjusted for the rate of population growth, which was about 2.8 percent, the growth of per capita income was only about 3 percent for the period. The low rate of inflation masks a number of major problems in the macroeconomic field. The extremely high dependence of the Cambodian economy on foreign economic and financial assistance is not sustainable.

Sectoral Weaknesses

Sectoral analysis also indicates that the growth performance in Cambodia during this period was not broadly based and was in fact precarious. For example the Cambodian economy is overwhelmingly dominated by agriculture. This sector represented on average about 45 percent of total value added during the 1991–95 period, but recently it has been gradually declining (see Table 2). During 1993–94, due to bad weather conditions rice and other crops recorded a decline and no growth. This, in turn, impacted negatively on the growth rates of real GDP during the same period. (See Figure 1.)

The service sector is the second-largest, responsible for about 35 percent of GDP. The construction and service sectors alone were responsible for about three fourths of GDP growth during 1991–95. The expansion in these sectors has been fueled by growing foreign investment and increasing numbers of visitors from Cambodia's more affluent Asian neighbors. However, the construction sector is highly dependent upon foreign investment and tourism—especially in a country with Cambodia's history— which is very sensitive to political conditions. Two events in July 1997—the currency crisis in Southeast Asia and the coup in Cambodia—are likely to have serious negative consequences for these two sectors, at least in the short to medium term.

The size of the industrial sector increased from 15.1 percent of GDP in 1991 to 18.7 in 1995, but the manufacturing subsector remained unchanged at about 7 percent throughout this period, and the construction sector's share represented about half of the total share of the industrial sector.

Mobilizing Resources

The government's large budget and balance of payment deficits have been extremely vulnerable because they have been financed almost entirely by foreign savings. On the revenue side of the budget, import duties represent an overwhelmingly large share of total revenue. On the expenditure side, military expenditures and government employees' salaries represent a very large share of the total, leaving very little for much-needed health, education, and other social expenditures. (See Tables 3 and 4.)

In a country like Cambodia, where there is a large surplus of labor, it is the availability of savings as a source of financing investment which determines the rate of output growth and productivity. The level of total investment as a percentage of GDP increased dramatically from 9.4 percent in 1991 to 21 percent in 1995. Both government and private investments recorded strong increases during this period. However, these investments were financed mostly by foreign savings, which increased almost tenfold, from a mere 1.5 percent of GDP in 1991 to 13.5 percent in 1995, rather than by domestic savings, which remained low, at an average of approximately 7.6 percent of GDP during this period. (See Table 5.) It is clear that without the large inflows of foreign savings, mostly in the form of multilateral and bilateral grants and concessional loans along with an increasing share of foreign direct investment, the economy of Cambodia could not have grown at the pace it did. (See Table 6.)

In 1996 the World Bank stated that for Cambodia to maintain an average rate of real growth of 7 percent per year for the next five years, a yearly average amount of $500 million in foreign financial resources would be needed to fund the balance of payments and budget deficits, service external debt, and allow for the accumulation of a critical minimum level of international reserves. These calculations were based on the fact that during the 1993–96 period, Cambodia had already received an estimated $2 billion in total economic and financial assistance from the international community.[9]

The extremely heavy dependence of the Cambodian economy on foreign economic and financial assistance is not sustainable. Therefore, the foreign savings must be replaced as soon as possible by domestic savings, as these sources of foreign financing will end sooner rather than later. The probability of success in mobilizing domestic resources will depend on reform policy measures that lead to the early establishment of, among other things, an efficient banking system, an open trading system, an efficient and transparent government, an efficient and transparent judicial and legal system, and a vibrant private sector.

The Quality and Sustainability of Economic Growth

The improvements in Cambodia's economy are a relatively recent development. For confidence in Cambodia's economy to be on more solid ground, one also needs to see whether the impact of this achievement is sufficiently broad-based and if the recent high rates of growth and price stability can be sustained over a long period of time.

In a country like Cambodia where the majority of the population still lives in rural areas and poverty and unemployment are high and pervasive, it is important to look also at the quality of growth that fosters human development, promotes equity, safeguards the environment, and allows an enhancement of the cultural values of the country. The quality of Cambodian performance is not satisfactory because the impact of the growth process is not broad-based. Economic benefits have been highly concentrated in the urban centers, especially Phnom Penh. At the policy level the containment of inflation has been achieved mostly through cuts in budget expenditures. Unfortunately these cuts have fallen mainly in the fields of educational, social, and health services, and they hurt those who need most—the poorest. At the same time military expenditures have increased, and the political will needed to reduce the bloated civilian and military bureaucracy has been absent.[10]

Institutional Foundations

The sustainability of Cambodia's economic recovery is threatened by severe shortcomings in the government's institutions. There is little political accountability in present-day Cambodia. The National Assembly exists largely to rubber-stamp policies rather than provide checks and balances. The bureaucracy, judicial system, and military, police, and security forces are highly politicized. Corruption is pervasive, demoralizing, and detrimental to good governance. There is not yet any fair and competent judicial system to decide disputes between locals and foreigners or the government and private parties.

Sustained economic growth requires that Cambodia's system of governance be made more transparent and efficient in delivering its services.[11] This requires an improvement in the legal and judicial system, civil and military administration, education system, monetary and fiscal system, accounting system, land titles recording system, private property system, labor organization, and foreign investment code. A host of legislation and other reform measures have been introduced. But one should remember that laws are only a framework to which people or institutions can refer in case of dispute or misunderstanding. The problems in Cambodia lie in the implementation.

Administrative reform is one key to Cambodia's becoming less dependent on foreign assistance and enhancing productivity. Civil, security, and military personnel represent about 4.5 percent of the total population of Cambodia, a very large proportion compared to other countries. They are also very poorly paid. The average monthly wage amounts to $25–$30, well below the subsistence level. Most civil and military personnel have a second job in order to survive. Therefore, Cambodia's productivity is very low.

This situation could lead to the loss of competitiveness in the export sector and an increase in corruption, which was already pervasive in Cambodia. Corruption can harm Cambodia's efforts to become economically prosperous and independent, as it diverts much-needed resources to support the rebuilding and rehabilitation of the economy. Moreover, it has a pernicious effect on society.[12]

The Cambodian government has had plans to gradually downsize its civil and military personnel with the help of external financing. However, there have been numerous problems in this endeavor. They are mostly political in nature, as both civilian and military personnel are highly politicized. Unless there is a strong political will, this problem will not be adequately addressed.

Another area of great concern to both Cambodians and the international community is the problem of resources management, forest management in particular. The opaque and unconstitutional method by which forest concessions have been granted to a number of foreign firms and the lack of control of illegal logging do not bode well for Cambodia. The rate at which the nation's forest reserves have been depleting is alarming. If this is not corrected soon, Cambodia's development prospects will be seriously jeopardized.

The Cambodian government plans to be more forceful in its environmental policy. During 1994 the government formulated a National Environment Action Plan in consultation with the World Bank and other donors. Again, this problem is not amenable to any quick solution as it is directly related to rent-seeking activities at the highest level of the Cambodian government. Only with monitoring and conditionalities from international financial institutions and major donors can this problem be contained if not resolved.

The elections scheduled for 1998 are a cause both for alarm and hope for many, Cambodians and foreigners alike. These elections will determine in which direction Cambodian society will move. If generally fair and free elections can take place, and if the outcome is accepted, then a new era of real hope and peace for the Cambodian people can begin. If not, there will be a period of great uncertainty, with possible social and political unrest, the consequences of which are difficult to predict.

Role of the International Community

The only meaningful oversight of the Cambodian government's management of the economy has come not from within Cambodia but from the international community. About 40 percent of the Cambodian government's budget expenditures are financed by IMF and World Bank programs as well as bilateral foreign assistance. The conditions attached to IMF and World Bank financial support enable these international financial institutions to monitor government actions that affect Cambodia's economy and to apply pressure when the government does not comply. Major bilateral donors increasingly have used international forums, such as the ICORC meetings to make the government more accountable vis-à-vis the international community and the Cambodian people. International NGOs also have been playing more major roles as monitors of the government's performance.

The coordination of official economic assistance to Cambodia and the monitoring of the economic reform program rests with ICORC. ICORC meetings are an important venue for the exchange of views among donors, the review of progress made, the raising of additional funds for the program, and the monitoring of the implementation of the program. These meetings also can provide major donors an opportunity to scrutinize and ask for changes or improvements in the program. Although implementation remains essentially the responsibility of the Cambodian government, monitoring is the responsibility of the donors and international financial institutions through contingencies and the phasing of financing.

Quantitative economic performance targets as well as a deadline for the introduction of institutional structural reforms were formally set and agreed upon between the Cambodian government and the international financial institutions in a letter of intent and a policy framework paper. It is within this framework, which is a kind of collateral, that the monitoring of the progress in the reform process takes place. Failure to meet the criteria of performance may lead to either a delay or a cancellation of the disbursement of funds. This framework provides a relatively good way to make the Cambodian government accountable for its actions and management and use of external resources.

Beginning in 1996, this monitoring process was used more forcefully. The turning point in this regard was the 1996 annual meeting of the IMF and the World Bank. During this meeting the two organizations for the first time officially and publicly warned their member countries that corrupt practices would no longer be tolerated. The granting of resources depends a great deal on whether or not these resources are used efficiently. Therefore, member countries cannot expect financial assistance if corruption is not checked or eliminated.

This new approach was quickly applied to Cambodia. At the Summer 1996 ICORC meeting in Tokyo, major donors insisted for the first time that the Cambodian government implement a more transparent forestry policy. This problem was so serious that the Socit General de Surveillance (SGS), a Swiss company chosen by the IMF to monitor logging activities in Cambodia, decided not to accept the job for fear of being involved in the dangerous game of party politics in Cambodia. In this context the IMF took the unusual measure of suspending further financial assistance to Cambodia until the forestry policy was clarified. And in September 1997, citing the government's inability to meet its economic conditions, the IMF announced that it had suspended its $120 million financial support program (of which $60 million had not been disbursed). To emphasize the seriousness of the situation, the IMF also decided to withdraw its resident representative in Cambodia. Following the IMF decision, the World Bank decided not to renew an $85 million budgetary support program until the IMF resumes its program.

The impact of the suspension of these programs goes well beyond their actual dollar amounts. The presence of the IMF in a country like Cambodia and the Cambodian government's willingness and ability to comply with the terms of its agreement with the IMF are important influences on the confidence level of foreign investors. The suspension of these programs will dampen the enthusiasm of all but the most adventurous investors.

There is a serious absence of institutions and groups inside Cambodia that possess both the vision and the authority to ensure that the government pursues economic policies that will result in broad-based, sustainable, and environmentally sound economic growth. Absent this, the international community, and particularly major bilateral donors, such as Japan, must continue to play a major role in encouraging the government to adopt the right policies and ensuring that they are implemented. This can best be accomplished through a nuanced use of carrots and sticks. But this approach must be coordinated carefully among donors, and underpinning any tactical compromises must be a firm commitment on the part of all donors to reject corruption, partisanship, and the further plundering of Cambodia's environment. Only if official donors and international NGOs adhere to this approach can there be any real hope for Cambodia to achieve sustainable economic growth and broad-based development.

Conclusion

It is generally recognized that during the Khmer Rouge's insane and brutal regime the Cambodian people lived through one of the most tragic and horrible experiences in recent history.. Perhaps this has had paradoxically beneficial and detrimental effects on the Cambodian people and their society.

On the beneficial side this tragedy has generated enormous and genuine sympathy and support from all levels of the international community. This has resulted in Cambodia receiving large amounts of economic, financial, and technical assistance since the 1991 Paris Peace Accords. It also caused the Cambodian people to become more aware of the world at large and to benefit from a cross-fertilization of ideas and ways of life. This has happened either through increased Cambodian contacts with foreigners in the country or through the exodus of Cambodians to countries and societies with new and different ideas and notions of entrepreneurship largely absent in Cambodia. There is little doubt that Cambodia benefited a great deal from those Cambodian expatriates who chose to return home to either to take advantage of new business opportunities, or to simply to try to help rebuild their shattered homeland.

On the negative side the plight of the Cambodian people could be a hindrance to quick recovery, self-respect, and self-reliance. Often, because of this unique and tragic history the international community has tended to be lenient regarding the standards used by the international community to assess the behavior and the performance of Cambodia's leaders. An example of this faulty reasoning is the frequency with which the Khmer Rouge regime is used as a benchmark to judge the success or failure of any economic, social, or political programs or the behavior of those in power. This amounts to the assumption that "anything is better." Thus the abuses of the basic rights of the Cambodian people by their leaders, which under normal circumstances would not be tolerated, are accepted.

On balance Cambodia's resource potential both in human and nonhuman terms is relatively good. For instance Cambodia does not yet have population pressure on land. Cambodia could have a food surplus with only slight improvements in the use of water and inputs such as fertilizers or mechanization supported by a good rural infrastructure and financing system. There are sufficient mineral deposits, including oil and gas, that can be commercially produced with the help, for instance, of foreign investment through the production-sharing contract system, as in Indonesia's case. With reform in the education system, Cambodia can eventually follow the example of other Asian countries that produce and export labor-intensive manufactured goods. Cambodia may soon join ASEAN and benefit not only economically but also in terms of political stability.

There is no doubt that since 1993 Cambodia has succeeded in laying a foundation for future economic growth. It has been transformed into a better place for at least some Cambodians but not for the majority. The Cambodian people are starting to emerge from a long, dark night. They urgently need warmth and light in their tragic and precarious lives.

Table 1. Major Macroeconomic Indicators, 1991–96

	1991	1992	1993	1994	1995	1996
real GDP growth rate	7.6	7.0	4.1	4.0	7.6	6.5
inflation rate	87.9	176.8	31.0	26.1	0.1	2.3
external sector balance (current deficit excluding official transfers as % of GDP)	-1.3	-2.5	-9.4	-13.7	-16	-13.9
budget balance (overall deficit as % of GDP)	-3.4	-3.6	-5.7	-6.8	-7.7	-7.4
money growth rate (M2 in %)	28.6	220	32.5	29.4	44.3	44.2
gross official reserves (in months of imports)	0.3	1.0	1.8	1.4	1.5	2.1

Source: International Monetary Fund, *International Financial Statistics.*

Table 2. Sectoral Share, 1991–95 (percent of GDP)

	1991	1992	1993	1994	1995
agriculture	51.8	49.4	46.9	45.1	44.7
industry	15.1	16.3	17.7	18.3	18.7
manufacturing	7.0	6.8	7.0	7.2	7.4
construction	6.7	8.2	9.6	9.6	9.9
service	33.1	34.4	35.4	36.5	36.6

Source: World Bank.

Figure 1. Relation Between GDP Growth and Agriculture

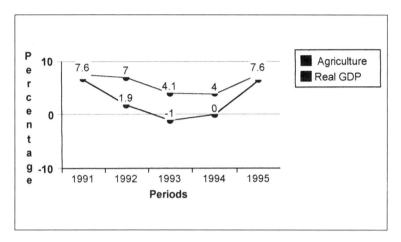

Table 3. Budget Expenditure, 1994–95 (percent of GDP)

	1994	1995
total expenditure	16.5	16.7
current expenditure	11.0	9.6
civilian	1.7	1.5
military	6.5	5.5
capital expenditure	5.5	7.1
locally financed	1.3	0.8
foreign financed	4.2	6.3

Source: Cambodian government.

Table 4. Tax Structure, 1994–95 (percent of GDP)

	1994	1995
total revenue	9.6	8.9
tax revenue	5.9	6.2
direct tax	0.1	0.3
indirect tax	1.2	1.4
trade tax	4.6	4.5
nontax revenue	3.7	2.7

Source: Cambodian authorities.

Table 5. Savings and Investment as Ratios of GDP, 1991–95

	1991	1992	1993	1994	1995
domestic investment	9.4	9.8	14.2	19.2	21.0
government	0.4	0.3	4.2	5.0	5.2
private	9.0	9.5	10.0	14.2	15.8
savings	9.4	9.8	14.2	19.2	21.0
national	7.9	7.3	8.1	7.4	7.5
foreign	1.5	2.5	6.1	11.8	13.5

Source: World Bank.

Table 6. External Financial Assistance (US$ million)

	1994	1995	1992–95	% Share
technical assistance	117	161	419	25
investment projects	123	169	392	28
budget/balance-of-payments support	69	7	222	16
food aid	12	4	81	6
emergency relief assistance	32	49	279	20
total	353	460	1394	100

Source: Cambodian authorities.

Notes

1. This portion of the paper draws heavily on the following sources: World Bank, *Cambodia: Agenda for Rehabilitation and Reconstruction* (Washington, DC: World Bank, East Asia and Pacific Region Department, 1992); Food and Agriculture Organization (FAO), *Cambodia Agricultural Development Options Review* (Rome: FAO Center for Investment, 1994); and Asian Development Bank (ADB), *Cambodia: An Economic Report* (Manila: ADB, 1991).

2. Statistical data on Cambodia are unreliable and therefore should be considered carefully. As of early1998,the most current economic statistics available were for1996.

3. Global Witness, *Corruption, War, and Forest Policy—The Unsustainable Exploitation of Cambodia's Forests* (London: Global Witness LTD., 1996).

4. UNDP, *Report of the Kampuchea Needs Assessment Study* (New York: UNDP, 1989).

5. Milton Osborne, *Before Kampuchea: Prelude to Tragedy* (Boston: George Allen & Unwin, 1984), p. 192.

6. IMF, *Cambodia* (Washington, DC: IMF Economic Review, 1994), p. 10. For a biased and sympathetic view of the Khmer Rouge regime, see George Hilderbrand and Gareth Porter, *Cambodia: Starvation and Revolution* (New York: Monthly Review Press, 1976).

7. United Nations, *The United Nations and Cambodia, 1991–1995* (New York: United Nations, 1995), p.148.

8. William Shawcross, *Cambodia's New Deal: A Report* (Washington, DC: Carnegie Endowment for International Peace, 1994), p. 15.

9. World Bank, *Cambodia: From Recovery to Sustained Development* (Washington, DC: World Bank, 1996).

10. For a good analysis of the impact of adjustment policy on income distribution and other social effects, see Lionel Demery et al., *Understanding the Social Effects of Policy Reform* (Washington, DC: World Bank, 1993).

11. On the role of the government in industrial policy, see Joseph Stiglitz, "Some Lessons from the East Asian Miracle," *The World Bank Research Observer,* August 2, 1996.

12. For a good understanding of the impact of corruption on the economy, see Poalo Mauro, "Why Worry About Corruption?" *IMF Economic Issues,* no. 6, 1997.

Rural Development in Cambodia: The View from the Village

Judy L. Ledgerwood

She has three children, two girls and a baby boy. Their life has been getting better, she says. They saved enough to buy a bit more land, so now they have just over two hectares. They have paid for their house plot and hope to save enough over the next two years to buy a raised wooden house. The thatch hut they live in now floods with the rains.

Life has been better since the 1993 elections because they have since stopped coming to coerce men into being soldiers. Her husband became a policeman to avoid the draft. This arrangement costs three chi of gold (about $150), but it worked only for about a year. "Why?" I asked. Because there were two bosses and only one received the money. The other had not, and so they fought. Her brothers are educated. She is the only one in the family who is illiterate. Her brother earned his Bac Dup (baccalaureate). Her relatives took him to Phnom Penh to try to attain a position in the bureaucracy, but it was far too expensive. It takes $3,500 to $4,000 to buy one's way in. Her mother sold part of her rice fields to pay, but the deal did not go through. So he has no position. Now her other brother, the young man who sits behind her (she pats his knee), has to pay to pass his exams for the eighth grade. They are worried that they will not have enough money to pay the bribes.

They are worried now, because of what they hear on the radio: FUNCINPEC accuses Hun Sen of this, Hun Sen accuses FUNCINPEC of that. They don't want to go back to war. They don't want the men to be taken away again. I try out my theory that the rich are so rich now that they will not be willing to live without the aid money, without the investment money. They stare at me unconvinced. "What do you know?" their expressions seem to say. What do I know? They have decided to keep more rice this year, to sell less, just in case. Rice stocks might see them through turmoil ahead. As we talk, she pulls the string that rocks a fat little baby boy in the hammock.[1]

Introduction

In most discussions of Cambodian political and economic development, the vast peasant majority, living at subsistence level, is generally invisible and silent. While "the people" are frequently noted in the Khmer press as supporting certain politicians or parties, very little has been written about life in rural Cambodia, and scant data are available for making policy decisions.

This chapter begins with three basic premises: First the vast majority of the Cambodian population lives in poverty in rural areas; second spending for economic development and assistance programs is unduly focused on the capital, Phnom Penh; and third, while rural development is touted as critical, the rural context and dynamics of rural development in Cambodia are inadequately understood. Given these facts the chapter addresses three topics. The first section reviews the scant data available about the lives of rural peasants based on recent research. The second and third address a number of the issues and debates that underpin efforts (or the lack thereof) to promote rural development in Cambodia. The final section makes preliminary suggestions for strengthening research on and the design of rural assistance programs in the Khmer countryside.

Rural Cambodia

Eighty-five percent of Cambodia's population lives in rural villages. Most of these people are rice farmers who practice one form or another of subsistence agriculture. Over 85 percent of the land under cultivation is in lowland rain-fed rice fields that produce an average of only 1.3 tons per hectare; average rice production per hectare is much higher in neighboring countries—over two tons in Thailand and over three tons in Vietnam. Food consumption is estimated at 260 to 290 kilograms of paddy per inhabitant per year, but in many areas with low soil fertility and high population pressure, farmers are unable to produce at these levels. Since 1990 harvest levels have been dramatically affected by drought and floods, particularly in 1991, 1994, 1995, and again in 1996. In 1997 flooding occurred again, particularly hard hit were Kompong Thom and Siem Reap provinces.

Land Ownership

Before 1975 land was privately owned. Land-holdings varied in size around the country, with an average of 2.2 hectares reported in 1961. Certain regions, most notably the northwestern province of Battambang, had areas of much larger holdings; but according to the 1956 Cambodian census, 55 percent of landowners had less than one hectare. In the village in Kandal Province where May Ebihara conducted research in 1959–60, 42 percent of the villagers owned less than one hectare of land, with most of the rest holding between one and two hectares.

Under the ravages of the Khmer Rouge during the Democratic Kampuchea (DK) period (1975–79), all agricultural lands were collectivized. The population was organized by age and sex into work teams that labored long hours at agricultural production and at the construction of a vast network of irrigation canals. During the course of the regime 1.5 to 2 million Cambodians died of exhaustion, malnutrition, disease, or were executed. Cambodian farmers' most bitter complaints about these times concerned rampant violence and the lack of food. They say they produced as much or more rice than they had before but were not allowed control over the product of their labors. While they starved the rice was taken away on trucks to feed soldiers and cadres or to be exported.

After 1979, with the establishment of the People's Republic of Kampuchea (PRK), a system of agricultural collectives known as Krom Samaki, or solidarity groups, was formed. Krom Samaki were composed of 10 to 15 families each. Each family was allocated a small plot for its home, while all other land was held as the property of the state. There were three official levels of collectivization, though there seems to have been greater variation from place to place. Level-one groups farmed as a collective and distributed the crop according to the number of persons in each family, with able-bodied workers receiving a greater share. Level-two groups divided up land and equipment among families (though all land was still owned by the state), but tasks such as transplanting and harvesting were performed by the group. Level three was essentially farming of private plots but with labor exchange among members of the group. The Krom Samaki were extremely unpopular and were eventually discontinued. Though they continued to exist on paper throughout the decade, most areas had quietly returned to farming private plots by the mid-

1980s—though with formal state ownership of property.

In spring 1989, with the withdrawal of Vietnamese troops at hand and negotiations under way for a settlement to Cambodia's civil war, the PRK announced a return to private ownership of property. In the land redistributions that followed, farmers were allocated between 0.1 and 0.2 hectares per family member, which meant land holdings ranging from 0.5 to 2 hectares per household. Holdings were divided based on residence in the village and land farmed since 1979 rather than any prerevolutionary claims to land. In some areas this distribution was conducted unfairly; local village, subdistrict, and district leaders received more and better quality land than other villagers. In the village where Ebihara conducted research in 1959–60 and again in the early 1990s there was evidence that considerable care was taken in how the allocation of land was made.[2] Since land was of variable quality, located at varying distances from water sources and so on, it was divided into small parcels so that individuals could have some good land and some of lesser quality. In this village landholdings are smaller today with an average of 0.68 hectare, as opposed to 0.88 hectare in 1960. In 1992, 79 percent of the villagers owned less than one hectare.[3]

It is also important to note that while the land distributions formally began in 1989, many farmers still did not have deeds to their property in 1996. In the 1993 election campaign, the Cambodian People's Party (CPP), the party of the old PRK government, ran on a platform that promised farmers titles to the lands they farmed. The CPP alleged that other parties would try to return lands to their pre-1975 owners. During 1992 and early 1993 cadastral offices around the country worked furiously to give farmers deeds to their lands to assure CPP votes in the elections. Yet many farmers still have only a piece of paper declaring that they have filed claim to a certain piece of land, not the final documentation verifying that such a claim has been approved.

Rural Communities Today

The first Socioeconomic Survey of Cambodia (1993–94) of the Ministry of Planning includes statistical data on rural households for the first time since 1962. But the survey provides only a hazy image of life in rural areas. The average household size in rural Cambodia is 5.4 people. An average of 20 percent of households are

headed by women. There are 88 men for every 100 women, a gender ratio more skewed than in urban areas. Thirty-one percent of
rural residents have completed less than one year of formal schooling. Eighty-two percent of rural households have no toilet.
Ninety-six percent cook with firewood; less than one percent have
electricity for lighting. Twenty-one percent have a radio, and nearly
6 percent have a television (this is higher than those houses having
access to electricity because the televisions are battery powered). The
percentage of household expenditures on food, beverages, and
tobacco in rural areas was estimated to be 67 percent of the monthly, total. Household income in rural areas is estimated to be less than
a third of the average urban household income.

With regard to social organization at the village level, we know
first that Khmer villages are highly variable. While the work of Éve-
line Porée-Maspero and others documented a high degree of social
and cultural variability throughout Cambodia before independence,
it is certainly even higher today. Some communities, particularly
those in the central and southern plains, are made up primarily of
the original residents who returned home after the forced population
shifts during the period of Democratic Kampuchea. In other areas
many residents remained throughout the DK years, but district leadership has been brought in from other areas. Elsewhere in the country, particularly where there has been fighting during the last 10
years, villages are made up of people who have fled other areas, who
were brought into the area as soldiers of whatever political faction,
who returned from the refugee camps in Thailand, and so on.
Obviously the sense of community in such areas is much less well
formed than that in the central plains villages, where people have
lived in relative peace since 1979.

Second, we know that with the return to private property and the
land redistribution of the late 1980s, differences in wealth are
reemerging. In the Kandal Province village where Ebihara and I conducted research, this differentiation is not yet as marked as it was
before the revolution. Ebihara notes that there were no socioeconomic classes within the village when she conducted her original
research in 1959–60, but villagers recognized relative degrees of
wealth among families based primarily on the size and number of rice
fields owned. She reports that in prewar periods there were more relatively wealthy people than those who were destitute. Today many are

considered to "have enough" (*neak kuasom*), meaning that they have enough rice to eat and possibly some surplus to sell, and there are fewer people in the top or bottom categories.[4] Those said to be "poor" (*kra*) include elderly people without able-bodied labor, female-headed households without male labor, and families struck by serious illnesses that incurred high medical expenses and loss of labor.

In some areas close to Phnom Penh a different phenomenon is occurring. Land speculators are buying up large tracts, anticipating the growth of the city. At the same time rising housing costs in the city center are resulting in urban sprawl, as the new poor occupy lands on the flood plain surrounding Phnom Penh, often as squatters. In areas where land has higher value, on the edges of urban centers and along the Mekong and Bassac rivers, numerous conflicts over land ownership have arisen. Most of the cases registered to the United Nations Transitional Authority in Cambodia (UNTAC) Human Rights Office in 1992–93 were cases related to land ownership. A common pattern during this period was for armed soldiers to appropriate at gunpoint tracts of land that were then divided into plots and sold to new migrants. Previous landowners were left with little or no recourse as local-level officials are unwilling or unable to stand up to armed force.

Third, we know that in some areas labor exchange (*provas dai*) and other forms of community cooperation are reverting to prerevolutionary patterns. At the same time agricultural production in other areas is characterized by cash payments for agricultural labor. This is the case in the Angkor Borei district, where farmers grow dry-season rice. Because the peak labor period is virtually the same for all farmers, there is neither time nor adequate labor to practice traditional exchange patterns. Hence farmers in this region hire large numbers of laborers, often from other districts.

Fourth, we know that some rural communities have taken it upon themselves to organize local nongovernmental organizations (NGOs) to encourage cooperative community activities, such as organizing ritual activity or working a communal field. Local NGOs that work at the community level are only beginning to establish themselves and become known to international organizations and possible donors.

The Urban-Rural Disparity in Development Assistance

While Cambodia's GDP grew at an average 5.9 percent from 1990 to 1995, these data include 20 percent growth in the urban and hotel sector and 15. 2 percent in construction. The rural sector in the same period was stagnant as rice production grew at -0.1 percent and livestock at 3.8 percent. Since the July 1997 coup d'état Ministry of Finance officials have revised estimates of economic growth for 1997 from 6.5 percent to 3 percent or less.

There is a similar pattern to the distribution of aid resources. Indeed most aid money, like most of the millions that poured into Cambodia during UNTAC, remains in Phnom Penh. Of the estimated $2 billion in total economic and financial assistance received from the international community between 1993 and 1996, the majority of funds did not leave the capital. This was obvious to an elderly woman in rural Kompong Speu Province, who in December 1995 asked me, "Why do you foreigners only give money to Phnom Penh?"

Examples from two areas, health and education, help to show the trends. The Ministry of Health received 6 percent of the national budget in 1994 and 8 percent in 1996. Donor assistance for health committed to date, however, focused on urban areas and on specific provinces. Phnom Penh, with 7 percent of the population, received 43 percent of the 1994 total donor aid for health and over 70 percent of the assistance for capital investment in the health sector, including construction of hospitals. At the provincial level aid was concentrated in three provinces: Kandal (where Phnom Penh is located), Battambang, and Banteay Meanchey (the provinces with the highest numbers of repatriated refugees). The central lowland provinces, home to more than two-thirds of the population, received only 21 percent of the aid.[5]

These efforts at the central level are arguably necessary before projects can be designed to reach rural areas. But the harsh reality remains that in most rural areas health care is nonexistent. The current medical system in Cambodia is renowned for being particularly profit oriented.[6] Though health care is theoretically provided by the state, in practice, no one is treated without cash payment in advance. Babies are delivered at home by traditional midwives. Maternal mortality rates were estimated at 600 per 100,000 live births in 1993; comparable statistics for Thailand in 1992 were 137 maternal deaths per 100,000 live births. Premature delivery and delivery complications cause about two-thirds of infant mortality. Nearly one-fifth of the children do not survive to age five. Where health care is available at the district level, it is often priced well beyond the means of the average farmer. Virtually everyone in rural Cambodia self-medicates with medicines available for purchase in the local markets.

Post-coup cuts in foreign assistance will worsen the health situation. The Ministry of Health reports that the cut in German aid will diminish the national pharmaceutical budget by approximately a third. This poses particular problems for the treatment of tuberculosis and malaria.

Government spending on education, about 7 percent of the budget in 1994, was up to 12 percent of the budget for 1996. In 1994 international NGOs funded about 48 percent of the total foreign aid to education, multilateral organizations about 35 percent, and bilateral donors about 17 percent. As is the case with the health sector most of this assistance was focused on Phnom Penh. Over 40 percent of this aid was absorbed by higher education. This means that not only is the aid restricted to Phnom Penh, where the institutions of higher education are located, but it is further focused on the male children of the wealthy elite, who can afford higher education for their offspring.

In 1993–94 only 15 percent of the student body at the University of Phnom Penh were women. Women constituted 12.6 percent of the students at the Royal University of Fine Arts, 12.6 percent of the medical school, 5.5 percent of the law school, 4.6 percent of the Agricultural Institute, and only 1.5 percent at the Institute of Technology.[7] While a decade ago it was possible for intelligent poor children to make it to university under a quota system established by the socialist government, this is no longer the case. Since the early 1990s admission and advancement at all of the institutes of higher learning are contingent on families paying informal fees to education officials.

Approximately 40 percent of the funding is directed to the primary level, which is the only level available in most rural areas. The typical primary school in a rural area serves two to three villages, and there is an average of only three secondary schools per district. Even more striking considering the problems of education in rural areas is the rate at which children drop out of school. Only 400 out of every

1,000 students who begin first grade complete all five years of primary school, and only 320 actually graduate. According to an Asian Development Bank (ADB) study, "approximately 80 persist to the end of lower secondary school and 60 to the end of upper secondary school."[8] The education system suffers from a wide range of problems, including lack of facilities, undertrained staff, lack of books and materials, low pay for teachers, and an ineffective curriculum.

Education is also priced beyond the means of many farmers. On the basis of a household survey the ADB concluded that "the government spends an average of 20,000 riels ($8) per primary student each year, while parents paid an average of 160,000 riels ($64), or eight times that amount."[9] Since teachers are not paid a living wage by the state, they must supplement their meager income by charging students additional fees to attend.

The government expenditures for agriculture in 1996 were only 4 percent of the total budget. Much of the aid for agriculture since 1993 has been in the form of funds for mine clearance and rural road rebuilding. Many of these projects were in areas of northwestern Cambodia where most of the repatriated refugees settled when they returned from the border camps.

A vast gap exists between central government ministry planning and activities and farmers' lives. Agricultural extension agents are trained but not deployed to rural areas. Government officials act in those areas where NGO or other aid funds are being expended but not in a generalized fashion. The new Ministry of Rural Development has plans for local-level representation and activities but has yet to establish local connections. It is difficult to say what impact the July coup will have on the plans of the Ministry of Rural Development and the Ministry of Education. The ministers from both were from FUNCINPEC and fled the country after the coup. They were replaced by two defectors from FUNCINPEC. The use of these positions as political payoffs does not bode well for any serious action being taken by these ministries for some time.

Except at particular development project sites there is virtually no connection between the ministries at the central level and rural residents. After the 1993 election of the coalition government, central ministries and provincial administrations were divided between the CPP and FUNCINPEC. But from the district level down no change has taken place. So today's district, subdistrict, and village leaders are the same ones from the PRK and State of Cambodia (SOC) period. Because of the conflicts and divisions between political parties and ministries at the central level of government along with those between personalities in ministries and at the provincial level, local-level rulers are left to rely primarily on their personal (mostly pre-1993) connections up the chain of command—or to run matters themselves.

Local elections scheduled for 1997 were canceled. Without any power sharing at the local level FUNCINPEC was reluctant to devolve control over, or funding for, development projects to the local level. There was a similar reluctance from within the CPP, since government structures throughout the PRK period were organized with power emanating from the central level. After the coup it is even more likely that the emphasis will be on top-down administration and maintaining political and economic control. In the short to medium term, there is virtually no chance that the focus will shift to allowing local level input on rural development projects.

Before the coup the need to grant project funding to rural areas was generally acknowledged, and planning for future socioeconomic development stated that this should be the case. Early in 1997 the National Assembly passed the First Socioeconomic Development Plan, 1996–2000, which focuses on rural development and poverty alleviation programs. The plan's goals for public investment, which will cost some $5 billion—almost three-quarters of which is expected to be financed from foreign sources—state that roughly 60 percent of the public investment needs to be allocated to rural areas. While this is an admirable goal, given the current political situation and cuts in international aid, there seems little chance that these plans will be carried out quickly, if at all.

Problems for Rural Development Planning and Implementation

The problems with designing effective rural development initiatives in Cambodia are complicated by the upheavals of the last 25 years. A 1995 ADB planning document listed some of the constraints on agricultural and rural development as follows:

> shortages of key inputs (water control, fertilizer, improved seed, credit, and transport); inaccessibility [due to] very poor rural infrastructure, including roads and communications, and a limit-

ed domestic market; insecurity, banditry, and land mines in several areas; a limited technical capacity in government departments, with a poor data base, ineffective research facilities and virtually no extension service; a skill base among the rural population limited largely to traditional subsistence practices, and with low literacy and numeracy levels; and a disinclination toward community or group action, aggravated by the memories of experience under the Khmer Rouge regime.[10]

This section addresses three of these concerns: the lack of available data on rural communities, the issue of correctly analyzing social relations with respect to organizing community development (often addressed in the development literature as a "lack of absorptive capacity"), and people's alleged lack of motivation to participate in development schemes. In the first instance the problem is very real; in the case of the latter, the Khmer context is little understood and the problems are overstated in the current literature.

Lack of Data

Written materials on rural village life in Cambodia before the upheavals of the last 25 years are scant. Far more research was conducted by Westerners, particularly French scholars, on the archaeological wonders of Angkor Wat and early Khmer history than on contemporary society. Most materials written in Khmer or French about prewar Khmer society that were stored in the country were destroyed during the years of war and revolution. Libraries hold only a fraction of the Khmer-language materials published before 1975, and ministries lack documentation of baseline data in their particular fields. Information exists as fragments, often only as oral knowledge.

The picture of rural life, as viewed from the city, is also skewed by the ongoing security concerns of the last 25 years. Before 1970 some Khmer traveled widely across the country to visit relatives in the provinces where their ancestors had been born, especially at the New Year and at Pchum Ben (the Festival for the Dead). During the civil war between Lon Nol's government forces and the Khmer Rouge insurgency from 1970 to 1975, large numbers of people fled rural areas to the cities to escape fighting. During the Pol Pot regime people were forcibly relocated throughout the country, mostly but not exclusively from urban centers to rural areas. People returned to the cities after Democratic Kampuchea fell, but given that many former urban dwellers had perished or fled abroad, most residents of Phnom Penh after 1979 were born in rural areas. Between 1979 and 1989 the movements of Cambodians were restricted, and many people who moved to urban areas did not subsequently travel extensively in the countryside—except for young men in the military—because it was widely believed to be too dangerous. While the perception of this danger changes over time with reference to particular geographical areas, it is my impression that, in general, urban Khmer today have far less firsthand knowledge of rural life. This began to change again in 1989 as NGOs started to undertake community development work at the village level, most employing urban Khmer staff for such projects.

Statistical information used by the government for policy-making, including census data, agricultural production levels, and reports of economic activities, usually originates at the district level. However, these statistics are often extremely unreliable and may be further distorted as they are consolidated further up the information chain to the central level.

After 1989 it became easier for foreigners to travel to rural areas, and in the early 1990s NGOs were permitted to hire Khmer staff. Consequently a series of small-scale studies were produced on subjects ranging from the state of rural hospitals to the problems of returnees. Other reports have focused on specific issues, from rural credit to education. These studies tend to be highly localized, focusing on only one or a few communities, and their conclusions are based on research conducted over a very short period, such as a few weeks or at most, a few months. They give us some snapshot images of life in particular places at particular moments, but it remains extremely difficult to extrapolate from these reports generalizations about Khmer social and economic relations in rural areas.[11]

The Debate over Village-Level Social Relations

The issue of the current status of village-level social relations has important implications for Cambodian and international efforts to promote development at the community level. This issue was raised in a paper presented at the July 1996 meeting of the International Consultative Group on Cambodia. It states:

The NGO Working Group on Community Development underscores as issues the lack of community cohesion and organization, the lack of participation of people in the development process, the inability of people to access resources and develop skills, the lack of cooperation among NGO, government, and local community groups, the lack of donor interest in long-term community development work, and the lack of security conditions necessary to ensure development.[12]

The reference to a "lack of community cohesion" reflects the widely held view that Khmer society has been significantly altered by the events of the last 20 years.[13] Society is seen as having become atomized; people are said to be willing to provide a smaller range of types of assistance and only to a limited group of people. John Vijghen has discussed this shrinking circle of relatives (*bong-p'oun*) and asserts that needy kin are often just given food so that they will not starve, but they are not given equipment, land to farm, or investment capital.[14]

Viviane Frings pursues this argument a step further, arguing that Khmer do not really care about each other any more, that they "have not learned anything from the socialist propaganda and organization." She writes:

when Cambodians do help, they always try to take some advantage out of it, even if the persons they help are their relatives. They do not help for free and do not think that they have a moral obligation to do it. They expect the persons they help to be grateful to them whatever the conditions of the help.[15]

Mutual aid, according to Frings, has become associated with forms of collective organization imposed by the state. She goes on to state that since there were no collective organizations at the village level in prerevolutionary Cambodia, Khmer peasants have not changed but rather returned to prerevolutionary patterns of not helping each other.

This school of thought, characterized by the work of Frings and often repeated by development workers in Cambodia, is carried to extremes in a recent study by Jan Ovesen and others entitled, *When Every Household Is an Island*.[16] Asserting essentially that the village is nothing more than a collection of houses, the authors conclude that these clusters do not constitute a socially or culturally significant entity, let alone a moral community. They write:

> The common picture is that the traditional social cohesion and self-help mechanisms in the villages that were destroyed under Pol Pot are now slowly returning to normal. There is an element of wishful thinking in this view, for it is questionable whether such a "normal," traditional social cohesion on the village level ever existed in the first place. It is less questionable, however, that the deterioration of social solidarity appears to be continuing still, and that it is reinforced by the liberalization of the economy and the consequent monetarization of most social relations beyond the nuclear family.[17]

This view of Khmer society is very seriously mistaken. Based on research conducted by Ebihara and myself, data collected in the village in which she first conducted research 30 years ago and revisited several times in the early 1990s, suggest that intravillage cooperation is still very much alive.[18] The bonds within a village are not those of artificially created "solidarity groups" but bonds of kinship. The only way to understand the connections that bind the residents of a village is to trace their bilateral kinship linkages (through both the husband's and wife's sides of the family) by birth and by marriage over several generations. Since Ebihara specifically focused on kinship relations and social organization in her original research, she is now able to trace these ties through three generations to understand the connections of each household to another.

Most of the inhabitants of this village returned to their native place after the upheavals of the Democratic Kampuchea period. Thus many have known each other since birth and are related to one another in some way, by blood or marriage. Most of the households in the village are connected not only by kinship but also by long-term friendships, with the complex reciprocal obligations that such relationships bring. They demonstrate a kind of tolerance for one another's personalities and habits that is found only in people who know each other well. Other communities, however, may be composed of those without such long-standing bonds.

It is true that the extreme violence and deprivation of the DK period made people watch out for themselves. But there is ample evidence from the village where we conducted research that people still help one another in a variety of ways, including sharing food, donating or lending cash, exchanging labor, providing emergency financial and other assistance, and giving psychological support. The social circles in which assistance is provided may have shrunk, but Ebihara and I interpret this as owing largely to villagers' limited resources—i.e., their restricted capacity to give money and land to others—rather than to a lack of concern for their neighbors. While limited material resources may reduce the number of people or the size of the circle of *bong-p'oun* that people might be able to help, our research indicates that Khmer "traditional" systems of mutual assistance and monitoring behavior are still active in this community.

Moreover the notion that the Krom Samaki agricultural collectives represented some kind of "real" community whose passing is to be mourned is not an attitude commonly expressed in Khmer rural communities. Quite to the contrary villagers, even the widows and other female heads of households whom the *kroms* were designed to help, consistently expressed a preference for a return to private ownership of property.

Contrary to the atomization school of thought, Khmer rural villages are interwoven communities capable of organizing for socioeconomic development programs. There is, however, a range of types of villages in different parts of the country, depending to a large extent on whether or not they reconstituted themselves with much the same prewar population after the upheavals of the DK period. I return to this point below.

Questions of Motivation

The issue of what constitutes a village is directly related to the common assumption among aid workers in Cambodia today that villagers will engage in development-project work only if they are paid. This is sometimes referred to as the "food-for-work" phenomenon. Since the World Food Program, Oxfam, and other agencies over the last decade or so have offered villagers food as payment for working on development projects, rural villagers are now said to balk at the notion of undertaking project labor without compensation.

That people won't want to work unless they receive some benefit in return is not a shocking concept. Gabrielle Martel's account of life in a village in Siem Reap Province in the 1960s includes two stories about the ability of villagers to organize for community labor. In the first case government officials ordered villagers to provide labor to repair a roadway. The roadway did not service their village, and they had nothing to gain from the project. The villagers sent a token group representing the village so as to appear to participate in the construction, while in reality doing as little work as possible. On the other hand Martel notes that when flood waters washed out a bridge that everyone used regularly to go to market, the villagers immediately organized a work group and repaired it.[19]

That thousands of rural communities all over Cambodia are in the process of organizing their meager resources and labor to rebuild Buddhist temples speaks volumes as to the villagers' abilities to accomplish goals they articulate themselves. By reconstructing temples, they are rebuilding the hearts of their communities and at the same time gaining Buddhist merit for this life and the next.

Much of this discussion about a lack of motivation on the part of villagers all too closely echoes French colonial visions of Khmer as indolent. If one is a firm believer in the intelligence of the common farmer, the logical explanation is that a refusal to participate is likely linked to a lack of interest on the villagers' part, a clear sign that the project was designed without the input or approval of the local population. It likely also reflects the villagers' belief that the only ones to benefit from such a program will be corrupt officials.

It is certainly not always easy to establish clearly what it is that communities want for themselves, or to motivate participation in development projects when farmers are already overworked and short of hours in the day. But it is also too easy to abandon this difficult task by saying either that there is in fact no community to serve or that people are unwilling to help themselves.

Conclusion

Given these problems the uncertainties of post-coup politics and the limited data that planners have as a base for designing national rural development policies, is it possible to make any statement about remedies? At present this may only be done in the most general terms.

First, some social development programs are best left entirely to the national government, and aid programs should directly fund the Royal Government of Cambodia (RGC) for these tasks. The most important areas are health and education. The Ministry of Health has strengthened its organizational structure and planning capabilities at the central level and has as its stated goal improving care at the district level, making it more available and affordable. For both the Ministry of Health and the Ministry of Education a key factor lies in their ability to pay a living wage to teachers and local health-care providers. Their services can be afforded by rural residents only if their cost is subsidized by the state in the form of adequate salaries.

Aid programs that provide funding for health, education, or agricultural services should not be cut. Cutting such funding does not hurt the Hun Sen government; it hurts poor Cambodians. The U.S. decision not to cut support for maternal and child health programs is a positive case in point.

Second, there is a clear need for more local-level research in conjunction with planning for development programs. Since rural villages vary greatly in terms of specific conditions, it is only logical that something that works in one area may not work in another. Before plans can be drafted for a particular area, research should be done in the region to try to understand community composition and characteristics.

Such research should be carried out by local researchers, who are most likely to be able to rapidly assess the social characteristics of the community. Therefore more training of Khmer social science researchers is urgently required. Support should be offered to organizations that train Khmer staff to conduct research programs for development. To date these include the Cambodian Researchers for Development, the Khmer Women's Voice Center, the Cambodian Development Resource Institute, and the UN Fund for Population Activities' work in conjunction with the Ministry of Planning to train interviewers for the 1998 census. Funding should also be made available for a limited number of Khmer to undertake graduate training abroad.

Other ideas to be considered would include linking higher education to requirements that young people provide a set number of years of service in rural areas after they finish their studies: as teachers, as health workers, and as agricultural extension agents. One way to facilitate this process would be to require that institutions of higher education recruit students based on a quota system, so that different areas of the country are represented. Graduates could then be required to return to their native areas to perform their years of service.

Certain other social development programs are best left to local organization and control. The best examples of these are the projects of small-scale local NGOs. While it is often difficult for international donors to identify successful local organizations, it is not impossible. Some international donors are already channeling funds to local NGOs, either directly or through international NGOs acting as intermediaries.

Two other endeavors are under way that merit further study for possible use as models striving to attain in form and content true community-based development. The first is the RGC's program called the Social Fund. Under this program local communities present projects they have designed themselves to funding agency representatives for approval. Social Fund program staff visit the sites and assess the viability of the projects, and a committee then decides on funding approval. Follow-up visits confirm that project work proceeds and that appropriate assessment is made at project's end.

A second program, funded by the UN Development Program, is a pilot project called Seila. In five provinces Seila strives to combine local participation and decision making with national-level policy-making. Development committees are elected at the village, subdistrict, district, and provincial levels. Province- and district-level committees are provided funding to allocate to worthy projects that are proposed from the bottom up. The idea is that if local-level committees express the opinions of their communities then development will be truly participatory. Each committee also has a number of slots reserved for women, thus assuring female participation in the decision-making process at every level.[20]

It is still too early to assess the success of these projects. While they sound ideal there is a strong likelihood that the newly created structures will immediately come to mirror the established patron-client structures that dominate Khmer political life. It is certainly simplistic to assume that forming a new committee through elections will automatically create a nonbiased and representative body. Local-level officials (almost all of whom are members of the CPP), their position strengthened by the July coup, are likely to resist strongly any activities that seem to threaten their exclusive authority.

The crisis at the national level means that the need to shift funding, focus, and control to rural communities will remain unaddressed into the foreseeable future. There seems little chance that central-level officials will concentrate their energies on Cambodia's rural communities, except in order to exert additional political control. It seems likely that community-based rural development programs will remain largely on hold.

In the face of the political upheavals of 1997 rural Cambodians are again hoarding rice, saving their money, and waiting for the storm to pass. Peasants interviewed in June and July 1997 did not express support for either political party; rather there seemed to be widespread resignation. Many people commented that widespread violence and political oppression were "normal" (*thommada*). Some dared to express a certain level of anger that their leaders continue to fight over power and will not let the people live in peace. Some quoted the Khmer proverb that says: "When elephants fight, it is the ants that get trampled."

Still the rebuilding of temples by communities all over Cambodia tells us that Khmer villages are capable of organizing for their own benefit. Cambodians, like most people, are cooperative when it is to their benefit. Rather than overidealizing an imposed form of collectivity from the recent past, development planners should focus on understanding the varying range of patterns of social organization in contemporary villages and tailor their efforts according to those specific conditions. Such specialized planning and program design is necessary if government funding and foreign development aid is to begin to reach beyond Phnom Penh to the 85 percent of Cambodians who live in rural villages.

Notes

1. Field notes, June 26, 1997, Takeo Province.

2. May M. Ebihara, "A Khmer Village in Cambodia" (Ph.D. diss., Columbia University, 1968), p. 221; "Beyond Suffering: The Recent History of a Cambodian Village," in *The Challenge of Reform in Indochina*, ed. Borje Ljunggren (Cambridge, MA: Harvard Institute for International Development), pp. 149–166; and "A Cambodian Village Under the Khmer Rouge, 1975–1979," in *Genocide and Democracy in Cambodia: The Khmer Rouge, the United Nations, and the International Community*, ed. Ben Kiernan (New Haven, CT: Yale University Southeast Asia Studies), pp. 51–63.

3. Judy L. Ledgerwood, *Analysis of the Situation of Women in Cambodia* (Bangkok: UNICEF, 1992), p. 47.

4. May M. Ebihara, "'Beyond Suffering': The Recent History of a Cambodian Village," in *The Challenge of Reform in Indochina*, ed. Borje Ljunggren (Cambridge, MA: Harvard University Press, 1993). See also May M. Ebihara and Judy L. Ledgerwood, "Economic Transformations and Gender in a Cambodian Village" (paper presented at the Northwest Regional Consortium for Southeast Asian Studies Conference on Southeast Asia and the New Economic Order, 1994). For a similar pattern in Pursat, see Paula Uimonen, "Responses to Revolutionary Change: A Study of Social Memory in a Khmer Village" (master's thesis, Stockholm University, 1994).

5. World Bank, *Cambodia: From Rehabilitation to Reconstruction* (Washington, DC: World Bank, 1994), p. 102.

6. See for instance, Willem van de Put, *Empty Hospitals, Thriving Business* (Phnom Penh: Mdecins Sans Frontires, 1992).

7. Secretariat of State for Women's Affairs, Kingdom of Cambodia, Report Submitted for the Second Asia and Pacific Ministerial Conference in Jakarta, June 7–14, 1994, and the Fourth World Conference on Women in Beijing, September 1995, pp. 34, 41.

8. Asian Development Bank, *Using Both Hands: Women and Education in Cambodia* (Manila: Asian Development Bank, 1994), pp. 16–17.

9. Ibid., p. 18.

10. Asian Development Bank, *Operational Strategy Study for the Kingdom of Cambodia* (Manila: Asian Development Bank, 1995), p. 21.

11. A considered effort must be made to preserve and utilize these small-scale studies. At least two libraries in Phnom Penh, at the Cooperation Committee for Cambodia (CCC) and at the Cambodia Development Resource Institute (CDRI), have collections of these valuable research reports.

12. Cooperation Committee for Cambodia, *NGO Statement to the Consultative Group Meeting*, July 1996, p. 5.

13. See first-person accounts describing the Khmer Rouge period, such as Haing Nor, *Haing Ngor: A Cambodian Odyssey* (New York: Macmillan, 1987). See also studies on the refugee camps in Thailand, such as Josephine Reynell, *Political Pawns: Refugees on the Thai-Kampuchean Border* (Oxford: Oxford University Refugee Studies Programme, 1989); Lindsay French, "Enduring Holocaust, Surviving History: Displaced Cambodians on the Thai-Cambodian Border, 1989–1991 (Ph.D. diss., Harvard University, 1994); and May Ebihara et al., "Introduction" in *Cambodian Culture Since*

1975: Homeland and Exile (Ithaca, NY: Cornell University Press, 1994).

14. John Vijghen cited in Viviane Frings, "Cambodia After Decollectivization (1989–92)," *Journal of Contemporary Asia*, Vol. 24, no. 1 (1994), pp. 50–66. Also personal communication.

15. Ibid., p. 61.

16. Jan Ovesen et al., *When Every Household Is an Island: Social Organization and Power Structures in Rural Cambodia* (Uppsala, Sweden: Uppsala University, 1996).

17. Ibid., pp. 66–67.

18. May M. Ebihara, "'Beyond Suffering': The Recent History of a Cambodian Village," in *The Challenge of Reform in Indochina*, ed. Borje Ljunggren (Cambridge, MA: Harvard University Press, 1993), pp. 149–66.

19. Gabrielle Martel Lovea, *Village des Environs d'Angkor—Aspects Démographiques, Économiques et Sociologiques* (Paris: Publ. de l'École Française d'Extrême Orient, 1975), pp. 263–64.

20. For more information on this project see, *Building the Foundation of the Seila Programme: The 1996 Work Plan of the Cambodia Area Rehabilitation and Regeneration (CARERE) Project* (Phnom Penh: UNDP, 1996).

Logging in Cambodia: Politics and Plunder

Kirk Talbott

Introduction

Cambodia's forests are a critical national asset for the country's political, social, and economic development. They provide tens of millions of dollars worth of annual revenue from logging, a wealth of biodiversity, and a range of ecological services. Cambodia's "Great Lake," the Tonle Sap, and the Mekong River, which are both central to the Cambodian economy and to the welfare of millions of Cambodians, are dependent upon surrounding forest cover.

In spite of the best efforts of many well-intentioned government officials, international and national nongovernmental organizations (NGOs), and thousands of citizens from local communities, Cambodia's forests today are under threat as never before. And, in many respects, the political and economic future of the country is held in the fragile balance between natural resource management and destructive plunder.

While accurate information about the current state of forests in Cambodia is exceedingly difficult to obtain, most estimates of forest cover in the country range from 30 to 40 percent, approximately one-half of what existed 40 years ago. Although some of Cambodia's forests are cleared by farmers obtaining household fuel and practicing shifting agriculture, deforestation is predominantly caused by commercial logging, much of it either illegal or uncontrolled. Cambodia already has one of the world's highest rates of deforestation and this is likely to accelerate, with 24 logging concessions covering almost 7 million hectares, approximately 40 percent country's area.

The list of ecological and socioeconomic problems associated with excessive logging and deforestation in Cambodia is long.

Landslides are increasingly common along many sections of river-banks, often causing the loss of dwellings and occasionally life. As rivers and lakes in the Mekong basin become shallower from siltation, heavy rains cause flooding in areas not ordinarily inundated. Conversely the shallowness of these same rivers and lakes causes them to dry up more quickly since water recedes more rapidly without the forest to act as an absorbent. There have been increasing reports of previously unknown storms in interior areas of the country where forests no longer act as natural barriers against strong winds.

Recent forest cutting around the Tonle Sap and the Mekong River has led to a disturbing reduction of fisheries. During the rainy season the inundated forest normally provides a system of root struc-tures that shelter the myriad of fish species as well as abundant food. Absent these trees fish populations in both lakes and rivers are decreasing. This trend has serious consequences for the future of Cambodia because fish is the main source of protein for its citizens. Deforestation is also causing serious water shortages in many parts of the country. These shortages are a threat to the welfare of Cambodia's rice farmers in particular and to the productivity of the agricultural sector in general.

The money that has been made from legal and illegal logging and the political influence that it represents is staggering. The offi-cial figure for revenue from timber sales between January 1996 and April 1997 was less than $15 million. However, the estimated value for logs and sawed timber exported or illegally sold within Cambodia is well over $100 million for the same period.[1] When the value of cut wood waiting in stockpiles along many rural Cambodian roads is included, the figure rises by nearly $30 million.

The plunder of Cambodia's forest is viewed by many as close to spiraling out of control. The resulting damage to the country's nat-ural resource base is huge, as is the loss of revenue to its government. And less tangible, but also important, is the concomitant loss of the government's credibility as the protector of the common good. As a result how Cambodia deals with logging is vital to the country's eco-nomic and political future. This chapter will look at the ecological and economic importance of Cambodia's forests, outline the politi-cal dimensions of logging since 1989, and provide scenarios for sus-taining this critical national resource.

Cambodia's Forests: A Critical National Asset

Cambodia has been blessed with an immense and rich forest cover. As recently as the early 1970s primary tropical forests covered much of the entire country. According to the World Bank, until the mid-20th century, forests totaled over 13 million hectares, or approximately 75 percent of the country's entire land area.[2] A report prepared by the UN Development Program (UNDP) and the World Wildlife Fund for the 1992 Earth Summit in Rio de Janeiro indicates that 73 percent of the country was forested as recently as 1965.[3] These figures suggest that Cambodia was one of the best-endowed countries in the world in terms of forest cover and the myriad of benefits this represented.

Cambodia's tropical forests have provided a wide range of important and beneficial ecological functions. They protect rich tropical soils, stabilize watersheds, and regulate water flows and local weather systems. They help prevent both flooding and drought— scourges of many tropical countries. The 1992 Earth Summit report for Cambodia described the country's "exceptional qualifications to develop as a 'green lung' of Southeast Asia."

Cambodia is particularly dependent on its forest systems given its hydrological makeup. The Tonle Sap, in the middle of the country, and the lower Mekong River represent a unique water system that plays a critical role in the country's and the region's economy and ecology. The lake is the largest freshwater body in all of Southeast Asia, with a surface area of 2,700 square kilometers in the dry season. For three months a year, starting in June, the increase in the volume of water in the Mekong River causes a reversal of the flow of the Tonle Sap River. During this time the lake acts as balancing reservoir for the flooding Mekong. This wet-season phenomenon is a fundamental cause of the immense flooded forest system around the Tonle Sap. It is an important contributing factor to the unique biodiversity of the ecosystem. The merging of freshwater and organic matter creates a richly productive biological milieu.

By virtue of this complex and unique system, the Tonle Sap provides a rich aquatic resource for fish production and rice farming, and, together with the Mekong, offers crucial hydrological functions to surrounding forest and agricultural areas. The system also harbors a great diversity and quantity of flora and fauna. Of great importance are the fish populations harbored in the Tonle Sap. Fish represents approximately 60 percent of the protein source for the people of Cambodia.

The forests surrounding the Tonle Sap, in turn, are essential to the effective functioning of the ecosystem. They protect the lake from siltation and eutrophication and play a predominant role in regulating the hydrology and water tables in the heart of Cambodia. Without the forests ringing the Tonle Sap, the fish population, the water level, and many other important natural features of the lake would be undermined to the detriment of the entire country.

Forests in Cambodia have perennially offered millions of Khmer villagers a vast array of local economic benefits. This is no small matter in a country ravaged by war, undermined by grinding poverty, and, until recently, long isolated from international assistance. In many provinces of the country, particularly in the heavily forested provinces of Ratanikiri, Mondonikir, Siem Reap, Preah Vihear, and Battambang, the forests provide many essential livelihood benefits, including materials for home construction, medicines, market goods, and a range of agricultural products and services.

Moreover many of the forests' benefits are difficult to quantify in tangible, economic terms. They are of profound historical and cultural importance to the Khmer people. Cambodian Buddhism places great value on the forest as part of the natural order of existence. Among Cambodia's many tribal peoples, especially in the northeast, local forests are central to world view and livelihood. They are seen as a source of both spiritual and material sustenance and are widely recognized as critical to protecting the soils, wildlife, and building materials of traditional societies.

At the same time forests are viewed as one of this impoverished country's most valuable economic assets, as well as an important source of revenue for the government. In purely economic terms the potential value of timber that can be utilized on a sustainable basis has been estimated by the World Bank and other groups to be at least $100 million a year. Given current patterns of rampant and illegal logging and the concomitant demise of forest resources, however, how much longer forests remain a Cambodian treasure is in doubt.

The Political Economy of Plunder: 1989–97

The fate of Cambodia's forests has been determined largely by the political situation within the country, as timber plays a critical role in determining the fortunes of the country's competing political and military leaders. Cambodia's timber stocks have been and continue to be exploited to finance the political and military rivalries that continue to plague the country.

Not surprisingly the political economy of logging in a poor, vulnerable, and conflict-torn country like Cambodia is largely shaped by the interests of domestic and foreign timber barons, influential politicians and government officials, and powerful military commanders. Time and again logging—or the ability to grant or withhold the opportunity to engage in logging—has been used to build personal fortunes, finance political activities, buy the loyalty of officials, and finance personal armies and the Khmer Rouge. Shadow economies based on illegal logging (as well as mining and narcotics trafficking) have proliferated across the country.

The Domestic Dimension

Reliable data is scarce, but many experts on forestry in Cambodia feel that the advent of the Lon Nol regime in 1970 triggered the country's first significant increase in deforestation. The political and economic corruption during this period (1970–75) set a precedent for resource extraction patterns without consideration of sustainability. Even less is known about logging during and immediately following the Khmer Rouge era (1975–79), but it may be that the rate of deforestation slowed owing to the combination of internal upheaval and international isolation.

It is clear that the pace of forest exploitation began to accelerate greatly in the late 1980s. The Hun Sen government, the Khmer Rouge and Thai military officers, and businessmen all engaged in the unsustainable cutting and export of Cambodian timber. In the rush to cash in on these forests, ideology and nationality were put aside and a complex set of rules of trade and finance developed around the cutting and sale of valuable species of tropical hardwood.

By 1992 there were reports of widespread and rampant logging throughout Cambodia. In June 1992 the *Far Eastern Economic Review* cited a UNDP estimate that 1.2 million cubic meters of logs—four times the amount of the year before—might be cut that year. According to the *Review,* "Past ravages may pale alongside the full-fledged attack on the forests now planned by the country's four once-warring factions.... [E]ach needs funds to prepare for next

May's election of a national government, and the forests provide an easy answer."[4] This situation was further exacerbated by the decision of the interim Supreme National Council in September 1992 to impose a moratorium on log exports. The moratorium was set to begin on January 1, 1993, at which time only processed wood could be exported from Cambodia. In anticipation of the moratorium logging intensified. The situation in late 1992 was aptly described by a knowledgeable Thai businessman who observed, "They are chopping away like mad."[5] And in early 1993 the *Washington Post* reported a burgeoning trade in logs between the opposing factions. "We're talking serious commerce," a well-informed diplomat said about cooperation between the central government and the Khmer Rouge. "This is not ideology. This is money in the pocket. They've got cooperative arrangements."[6]

Given the isolation and dangerous conditions that existed at that time in much of the countryside, particularly in remote forest areas, it was nearly impossible to document the players and arrangements involved in this plunder. Clearly, however, all three of the major political forces vying for control of Cambodia—Hun Sen's Cambodia Peoples' Party (CPP), the royalist FUNCINPEC party, and the Khmer Rouge—were deeply involved in logging in the areas they controlled. The Khmer Rouge, who ended up not participating in the 1993 elections, were estimated to be making between $10 million and $20 million a month on logging in areas they controlled. Only since the defection of Ieng Sary and the disintegration of the Khmer Rouge as a military force have the guerrillas been forced to relinquish their control over much of the timber and logging in northwestern Cambodia. It is important to note, however, that as of late 1997 large areas along the Thai border rich in timber and gems remained under the effective control of the remnant factions of the Khmer Rouge.

The International Dimension

There were other groups reaping even larger profits from Cambodia's vulnerable forests. The web of arrangements among the various Cambodian factions has entailed the complicity of many individuals and groups from Thailand, Vietnam, and other Asian countries. In the period between the signing of the Paris Accords in October 1991 and the holding of elections in May 1993 the rampant exploitation of Cambodia's valuable and vulnerable forests in a trade with neighboring countries began in earnest. With the end of Cambodia's isolation after almost two decades, businesses in neighboring and other countries began to take great interest in its forests and other exploitable resources, particularly minerals and gems.[7]

The economic stakes in this timber trade are high indeed. According to some reports, foreign companies have paid as little as $40 per cubic meter to the Cambodian government for valuable tropical species. The World Bank has determined the minimum fair economic rent for Cambodian timber—that is, what the RGC should charge concessionaires—to be $75 per cubic meter. This wood can be worth several hundred to a few thousand dollars per cubic meter on the world market. At these prices the estimates of standing stocks of timber ready for harvest and logs awaiting transport from stations are in the hundreds of millions of dollars.

Thailand, once a famed exporter of teak and other tropical hardwoods, has played a major role in extracting timber from its mainland Southeast Asian neighbors since the early 1980s. Thailand's rapid economic growth caused it to suffer some of the world's highest deforestation rates during the 1970s and 1980s. Since the early 1980s Thailand has had to import increasing amounts of timber to satisfy its rapidly growing domestic demand for construction materials and furniture production. In 1989, after flooding and landslides caused by deforestation led to hundreds of deaths, the Thai government imposed a belated logging ban. To make up for their deficit in timber supplies, Thai businesses, with the backing of their government, have increasingly sourced timber from Cambodia, Laos, and Burma.[8]

Yunnan Province and the rest of southern China also play an important role in determining the demand for Cambodia's timber. China's population and the recent rise in the economic status of its citizens creates an enormous demand for Southeast Asia's forests and other natural resources. Cambodia does not border China as do Burma, Laos, and Vietnam. However, the close relations between the two countries, the many ethnic Chinese businessmen who live in Cambodia, and the vulnerability of Cambodia to its larger neighbors make for a strong Chinese influence on logging and other economic enterprises.

In the two years following the 1993 elections 11 foreign firms were given logging concessions totaling approximately 2.4 million hectares. The most prominent of the international logging companies gaining access to Cambodia's forests were the giant Samling Corporation of Malaysia and the Indonesian Panin Group. In August 1994 Samling was granted an 800,000-hectare concession, approximately 4.5 percent of the entire area of Cambodia. In summer 1995 the Samling deal was dwarfed by the Panin Group concession of 1.5 million hectares. At the end of 1997 just under 7 million hectares had been allocated as concessions.

International involvement in the logging of Cambodia's forests has not been limited to the Thais, Chinese, Malaysians, and Indonesians. There have been repeated reports of Japanese, Taiwanese, French, Korean, and U.S. companies becoming involved in logging ventures. Vietnam and Laos share long and porous borders with Cambodia, and their military forces, in particular, have been involved in a number of logging deals. Global Witness estimates that a minimum of 260,000 cubic meters of logs, worth $130 million were illegally imported to Vietnam in 1997 and early 1998. According to Global Witness, all of those exports took place with the complicity of senior Cambodian officials and the Vietnamese military. Reports in 1997 suggest that Laos is taking effective action to arrest the flow of illegal logs crossing its far southern border.

Domestic and International Responses

Mok Mareth, the minister of environment, has been a principled and vocal critic of the country's deforestation "catastrophe," predicting the demise of Cambodia's forest resources within years. The last three and a half years have witnessed a near frenzy of political pronouncements from the Royal Government of Cambodia (RGC), logging bans, and sanctions against illegal logging. At the same time, however, logging deals and deforestation have proceeded at an equally feverish rate.

Particularly controversial was the government's decision in June 1994 to give control of timber exports to the Ministry of National Defense. This grant was part of an ill-conceived strategy to use timber revenues to finance the Royal Cambodian Army's campaign against the Khmer Rouge. An official of the newly formed Environmental Secretariat (which was to become the Ministry of Environment) warned that "this move is dangerous for democracy and the government's stability."[9] Some elements within the newly constituted government took a stand against the continued plundering of Cambodia's forests. In October 1994 the Ministry of Finance sent a confidential memorandum to King Sihanouk in response to "new procedures" authorized by the two co–prime ministers to grant exceptions to the logging ban of 1993. The memorandum states:

> These new procedures gave exclusive authority to the two prime ministers to approve any export license at the request of the Ministry of National Defense. The subsequent decisions of the prime ministers have shown a high degree of irresponsibility and inconsistency leading to considerable confusion and bringing about a huge loss of revenue to the state and very serious damage to the environment.

The minister of finance, Sam Rainsy, eventually resigned from his position in the government, in part in protest over the illegal logging and the siphoning of tens of millions of dollars in logging revenues from state coffers.

The government's unwillingness or inability to control logging became an issue for the international donor community for financial as well as ecological reasons. After the 1993 elections the international community made sizable commitments of financial and technical assistance to Cambodia. Nearly half the 1994 government budget, or about $170 million, was funded with foreign assistance. When the donor community became aware of the magnitude of logging revenues being diverted from the national government—and the pervasiveness of the corruption that made this possible—it began to express concern. The International Monetary Fund (IMF) was the first international organization to respond to the diversion of logging revenues from the Ministry of Finance to the Ministry of National Defense. In November 1995 the IMF postponed making a $20 million loan to Cambodia, citing inadequate forest management and protection and the government's failure to channel official logging fees to the central budget.

Reports by the British environmental NGO, Global Witness, and stories in the *Phnom Penh Post* and the *Far Eastern Economic Review* underscored the scope and seriousness of Cambodia's corrupt logging practices. Global Witness, which has played a leading role in mobilizing the international community to take action, joined with other groups to successfully persuade the U.S. Congress to toughen the U.S. stance on the Khmer Rouge and force Thailand to tighten its border controls. In February 1996 Global Witness exposed "documents signed by Cambodia's co–prime ministers permitting 18 Thai companies to export 1.1 million cubic meters of felled timber, mostly from Khmer Rouge territory."[10] This was an extraordinary event, since the potential revenue of this deal represented approximately $380 million, more than 50 percent of the entire Cambodian national budget.

This exposé led to a freezing in May 1996 of the $20 million IMF loan that had been postponed in November 1995. A June 1997 Global Witness report described the situation in Cambodia as

> at a crisis point with illegal logging escalating at an alarming rate. Legal concessionaires are illegally cutting both inside and outside of the country; timber is flowing into Vietnam and is being exported by sea; and vast revenues are being diverted into a parallel budget. Most of these activities are carried out with the active support of the co–prime ministers.[11]

At the July 1996 meeting of the international donors engaged in Cambodia, a number of the 21 delegations pressed the Cambodian government to address the logging crisis. Some called for a ban on log exports and a review of logging concessions. The World Bank initiated a series of detailed studies of forest management in Cambodia. The Cambodian government promised action. But absent a change in the political environment or a genuine commitment to curb corruption, there was little cause for optimism.

On December 31, 1996, in response to growing international pressure, the co–prime ministers promulgated a decree banning the export of all logs. However, this was and remains a decree—not an act of legislation—and there is little evidence that it has slowed the flood of illegal exports. The decree was followed by RGC Decision No. 17 in April 1997, which continued the ban on the export of round logs but legalized the export of rough cut logs if they were from legal concessions in licensed cutting areas and exported through exit points designated by the RGC. According to Global

Witness, the co–prime ministers continue to authorize "virtually every concession and illegal timber export" and the Royal Cambodian Armed Forces conduct logging operations anywhere they choose, "including legal concessions, national parks, and forests devoted to community use." Moreover, the Department of Forestry is denied access to many concession areas, making forest management impossible.[12]

The Current Logging Drama: Challenges and Opportunities

With the elections scheduled for July 1998 looming large on the political horizon, Cambodia's forests continue to play a pivotal role in financing political and military outcomes. Not much has apparently changed in terms of ongoing and, in many areas, unchecked logging throughout substantial areas of Cambodia. If anything, given the halving of Cambodia's forest stocks in recent years, those areas of valuable timber still standing are more valuable than ever, and the pressure to cut and sell mounts. A Cambodian official recently noted that the demand for timber in Kompong Cham was so great that illegal loggers had begun to cut down trees in the rubber plantations.[13] At the same time, although the logging problems in Cambodia may appear overwhelming, especially in terms of recent trends, there are abundant resources and a growing reservoir of experience, interest, and good will to draw on to turn the current situation around.

Positive Developments

There continues to be an opportunity for identifying and perhaps addressing the root causes of rampant and destructive logging in Cambodia. To begin with information is power. In Cambodia the power of the press—particularly the foreign press—remains considerable though tenuous. The *Phnom Penh Post* and the *Far Eastern Economic Review* have provided in-depth coverage of the political and economic dealings related to logging Cambodia's forests. Their stories have exposed logging deals, scandals, and environmental degradation in Cambodia. They have been joined by other foreign media, particularly Thai English-language newspapers, such as the *Bangkok Post* and *The Nation*. Thailand's own recent experience with environmental degradation and consequent flooding and localized drought has made deforestation a hot topic.

Another positive development is that the logging situation in Cambodia has taken on an overtly political veneer since Sam Rainsy quit his post in 1994. He has formed his own political party, the Khmer Nation Party (KNP) and made the issue of the country's deforestation an important plank of his party and his campaign. Whether the 1998 elections will include the issue of logging will depend, in large part, on the success of Sam Rainsy's campaign and if his commitment to sustain Cambodia's forests is adopted by other political leaders. Sam Rainsy was nearly assassinated on March 30, 1997, during a peaceful demonstration on the steps of the National Assembly in Phnom Penh, by a grenade attack that killed 20 of his supporters and injured 150. Evidence collected by the FBI is said to implicate elements in the CPP and military.

Mok Mareth also has continued to take an active and sometimes bold stance on trying to arrest illegal logging in Cambodia. Although his ministry is relatively weak compared to others, he has been able to effectively draw attention to the problem and take limited action. For example, the U.S. ambassador joined him in flying over areas of illegal logging inside of one of Cambodia's new national parks. The minister appealed successfully to the highest levels of government to have the logging operations shut down. With support from USAID and other bilateral donors, NGOs, such as the WWF, the UNDP, and other international agencies, the Ministry of Environment has matured rapidly and is in the process of developing some significant institutional and technical capacities in forest monitoring, park planning, and environmental education, among others.

There is a nascent National Committee on Cambodia's Forestry Policy that provides an institutional base for interagency collaboration in forestry, although it remains to be seen how effective or politically viable the committee will be—particularly since the July 1997 coup. The Royal Government of Cambodia, with encouragement from the World Bank, among others, is pursuing a program with four major assistance assignments: management of forest concessions, development of forest-policy process, legal review of forest utilization contracts, and log monitoring and verification. Each area is key to Cambodia's developing an operational, effective, and sustainable forest-management system.

The situation in the provinces remains tenuous, and control is often out of the hands of the central government. But there have been important recent steps in the right direction. For example, the Asian Development Bank, UNESCO, international environmental NGOs, and some community groups are joining with the Ministry of Environment to improve natural resource management and planning for the Tonle Sap.

The experiences of other Southeast Asian countries and regions of the world have shown that community-based resource-management systems are successful in protecting forests from uncontrolled logging and agricultural conversion. Granted tenurial rights as an incentive to responsibly manage local natural resources and assets, residents of forested areas often prove to be the most effective stewards and enforcers of sustainable forest management. While there are very few, if any, indigenous, forestry-focused Cambodian NGOs, a small but effective group of international NGOs has introduced community-based forest management in Cambodia. The Mennonites, for example, have worked for several years on building community-based forestry initiatives with some on-the-ground success in forest regeneration. A growing number of individuals and communities are taking a stand to protect their local forest resources. However, they face a long, uphill battle against powerful businessmen, government officials, and military officers who are prepared to use any means to gain and exploit forest concessions and discourage community-based activism.

Finally there is a trend toward a more aware and aggressive stance on environmental issues by many of the donor countries that comprise the International Consultative Group on Cambodia (CGC). In the 1996 and 1997 meetings of the CGC, representatives of the donor countries were outspoken in tabling their concerns. Moreover some groups are campaigning with some effect to use more leverage in the CGC process to drive reforms in the logging sector. Global Witness has asserted that "the economic leverage currently possessed by the international community is possibly the only factor that can influence the RGC's future approaches ... to the logging crisis."[14] They may well be correct given Cambodia's recent history, current tensions, and the nascent nature of the government's structure and the rule of law.

A Logging Ban?

A key debate concerning forest management in Cambodia revolves around the question of whether or not the RGC should impose a national logging ban. Global Witness advocates the enactment and enforcement of an immediate logging ban as the first goal for Cambodia's forest policy. According to this argument the current situation in Cambodia is altogether unacceptable in terms of protecting the country's forests for future generations, and a stopgap measure is required. In a June 1997 report, Global Witness unreservedly recommended that the RGC immediately suspend all concession activity and halt all exports of logs and processed timber until the World Bank–funded technical assistance projects are put in place and completed.[15]

The World Bank takes the stand that a logging ban is not the answer to Cambodia's unsustainable logging travails. Instead it advocates a policy framework for sustainable-forest management to be put in place with the requisite enforcement capacities and mandate. Realistic or not in a country as volatile as Cambodia today, the approach presented in the bank's 1996 Cambodia Forest Policy Assessment is based on extensive international experience and careful in-country financial and policy analysis. The assessment proposes policy initiatives and specific technical and financial interventions that can ameliorate the current economic conditions driving excessive logging. It offers several strategic actions backed by the assurance of financial and institutional support given government commitment.[16] These include:

- legal advice on existing concession contracts to resolve many outstanding financial and forest-management problems;
- technical assistance to improve criteria for evaluation of concession master plans drafted to ensure compliance on implementation features of forest concessions; and
- the preparation of detailed terms of reference for a concession and log-export control policy to help realize the enormous fiscal benefits estimated to be available from revising concession policies and controlling log exports.

While these and other multilateral organizations' prescriptions are highly technical in nature, they are broad-based and potentially significant in implication. For example the bank's forest policy assessment represents a large-scale collaboration among the government of Cambodia and the World Bank, the UNDP, and the Food and Agriculture Organization—if nothing else a promising sign for Cambodia given its recent history of isolation. The assessment represents not only the beginnings of political will, albeit on the part of only a few key government leaders, but also the financial resources to support in full the recommendations offered in the document. But the World Bank and other international organizations are constrained by the limitations of the UN system and the requirements of working with government agents whose intentions might not be legitimate.

An international forestry expert, Gerry Hawkes, provides a counterpoint to the World Bank's prescription for the current challenge of addressing logging in Cambodia:

> To put it bluntly, suggestions for improved concession management and harvesting are virtually pointless given the widespread corruption, civil unrest, and the vested interests in escalating illegal timber harvesting. Given an ideal political situation, there are many management and harvesting techniques which can be introduced to minimize resource damage and maximize societal benefits from timber exploitation, but none are truly sustainable at the levels of exploitation demanded by modern economies, particularly in countries plagued by the historical and political dilemmas of a country like Cambodia.[17]

Many people familiar with the challenge to sustainable-forest management of overcoming political and commercial constraints would agree with Hawkes' analysis and recommendations. He is joined by many others in advocating the transformation of many forested areas in Cambodia into community-based resource-management areas. Only after the functioning rudiments of civil society and commerce are in place can Cambodia responsibly open up to foreign concession arrangements.

Conclusion: Future Scenarios

Cambodia is at a critical moment. Enough of its original forest cover is intact that, given appropriate policies and actions now, its forests could be logged for decades to come while providing tens of millions of dollars in revenue to the nation's government and citizens. Crucial ecological functions provided by biologically diverse forest cover and necessary for sustainable development can still be maintained. Much progress has been made in developing the political awareness (if not political will) and technical and financial assistance (if not capacity) to manage this precious national resource. International pressure has had a substantial impact on the situation along the Thai border, the demise of the Khmer Rouge is promising, and the World Bank, Global Witness, and other international organizations continue to work constructively and effectively on these issues.

In 1997, however, the shattering of the fragile political coalition and the resulting damage to the Cambodian economy do not bode well for the transparent management of Cambodia's forest resources. According to a June 1997 World Bank report, there is

> a continued granting of forest concessions, annual harvesting licenses and authorizations for collection of logs outside concession areas. These awards are not market-based, transparent, or based on satisfactory technical, environmental, or other assessments. This is clearly inconsistent with the RGC's adoption of the strategy recommended in the *Forest Policy Assessment* and should therefore cease.

The next couple of years may well be critical to determining the fate of Cambodia's forests. While one cannot predict the future—especially during this particularly uncertain time in Cambodia—the following three scenarios are directions the country could take in terms of logging and forest management.

Scenario 1: The Worst Case
This scenario assumes that either Cambodia descends into civil war or essentially authoritarian elements remain in control of the government. This would likely result in a serious decline in foreign investment and economic assistance. In this crisis environment the value of Cambodia's timber would increase and the domestic and international constraints on plunder would be reduced. Rampant logging would accelerate in some areas. (When the IMF threatened

to withdraw its $20 million loan in 1996 Hun Sen threatened to simply sell off Cambodia's remaining forests.) A few protected areas and parks would be showcased to the international community; however, the country would be effectively cleared of its remaining forest areas leaving less than 10 percent forested within 10 years.

Severe ecological damage would ensue, including the collapse of fisheries in the Tonle Sap and much of the Mekong and its tributary system. Desertification could begin in significant swaths of the country, and rice and other key agricultural product levels would plummet. Poverty, inequity, and civil unrest would be exacerbated. Cambodia would be reduced to a beggar state despite billions of dollars worth of multilateral and bilateral foreign assistance.

Scenario 2: The Mixed Case
In this scenario it is assumed that credible elections are held in Cambodia, a new government is formed (perhaps another shaky coalition), and there continues to be a degree of political pluralism and openness. This would result in increased political stability and renewed foreign investment and aid flows. An improvement in the economy would reduce the need to engage in logging. But as long as Cambodia's political leadership feels compelled to keep their bank accounts and war chests well stocked—and can do so with impunity—Cambodia's forests will be vulnerable. The boundaries between legal and illegal forest extraction would continue to be blurred. Various rogue factions and the more mainstream political and military forces would continue to control different logging areas and operations. There would be some success in slowing the illegal, rampant logging that has taken place along so much of the Thai border area, particularly during the last decade. Over the next decade the remaining forest area would decline to 10 to 20 percent of the country, from the current 35 to 40 percent. As a result there still would be severe ecological and socioeconomic implications. The people hurt most would be the country's predominant population of villagers and farmers.

Scenario 3: The Best Case
This scenario assumes the emergence of a coalition of political forces committed to democracy, good governance, and sustainable natural resource management. Existing logging concessions would be

reviewed and canceled or changed based on sound management practices and the rule of law. A new set of logging concessions would be implemented along the legal, financial, and operational lines suggested in the World Bank's *Forest Policy Assessment*. Illegal logging would be largely stamped out by the new government in concert with local communities. Thousands of communities across the provinces would act as stewards of their local forest resources with support from a variety of government ministries and agencies. Cambodia's bloated armed forces would be reduced, and many of these soldiers would be retrained to monitor and protect the country's forest resources.

The Cambodian and international press would provide a steady stream of accurate information regarding natural resource use in Cambodia and the regional dimension to resource extraction and trade. This reporting, coupled with the reports of domestic and international NGOs, would foster the increased involvement of the international community. International donors would coordinate to support legitimate forest management policies and practices. Foreign assistance would include substantial equipment, training, and capacity building for forest management. Significant income would be generated for national government coffers as well as for local communities.

...

Many individuals and organizations inside and outside of Cambodia are trying to move the country in the direction of the third scenario. The roles played by Cambodia's neighbors and the international community are key to the future of Cambodia. It is hard to imagine how Cambodia's forests can be saved for future generations without the implicit or at least partial support of Thailand, Vietnam, Laos, and Malaysia as well as Japan, China, and the United States. The Cambodian diaspora in America, Europe, Australia, and elsewhere is an important constituency in this regard.

The many constructive contributions of Cambodia's citizenry, well-intentioned government officers, and representatives of the international community promise at least the possibility of an improved forestry situation. The stronger the political elite's adherence to the rule of law, the more vital Cambodia's civil society becomes, and the healthier its economy, the better the human and institutional environment becomes for forest management and logging that is neither rapacious nor destructive.

Notes

1. "Just Deserts for Cambodia: Deforestation and the Co–Prime Ministers' Legacy to the Country," (London: Global Witness, June 1997), p. 3.

2. World Bank, *1996 Cambodia Forest Policy Assessment* (Washington, DC: World Bank, 1996), p.3.

3. John V. Dennis and Gregory Woodsworth, *Report to the UN Conference on Environment and Development: Environmental Priorities and Strategies for Strengthening Capacity for Sustainable Development in Cambodia* (Washington, DC: World Wildlife Fund, April 1992), p. ii.

4. "Cambodian Assault," *Far Eastern Economic Review,* June 4, 1992, p. 64.

5. "Thais Blamed Most for Rape of Forests," *Bangkok Post,* November 15, 1992, p. 1.

6. "Phnom Penh Said to Undercut UN Effort to Save Forests," *Washington Post,* February 3, 1993, p. 11.

7. For several specific examples of foreign concessionaires, RGC officials, Khmer Rouge cadres, and Thai military officers involved in a series of timber cutting and exporting ventures, see "Forests, Famine, and War—The Key to Cambodia's Future" (London: Global Witness, March 9, 1995).

8. Burma offers one of the most compelling parallels to Cambodia in terms of the political and economic underpinnings to logging patterns and rates. Burma holds almost 50 percent of the remaining forest cover in Southeast Asia. In recent years, however, its forests have been threatened, primarily by the intensive regional demand for its teak and other valuable hardwoods. Between 1989 and 1993 over 30 concessions were granted by the military regime to Thai businesses. By the time that these concessions were canceled, much of the county's southeastern forests had been largely degraded. In the last several years logging has tripled along the Chinese border, and there are reports of accelerating cutting along the vast Indian border and the southern border with Bangladesh. Deforestation rates nationwide have doubled, with most of the timber being exported illegally. As is reported to be the case in Cambodia, heroin is often exported on logging trucks. Burma holds approximately 70 percent of the world's teak and dominates the heroin export business, providing some 60 percent of the world's supply.

9. *Phnom Penh Post,* July 29–August 11, 1994, p. 3.

10. "Activists at Loggerheads with Timber Traders," *Asian Business,* April 1996, p. 11.

11. "Just Deserts for Cambodia: Deforestation and the Co–Prime Ministers' Legacy to the Country" (London: Global Witness, June 1997), p. 30.

12. "Going Places ... Cambodia's Future on the Move" (London: Global Witness, March 1998), p. 3.

13. "To Control Cambodia, Rivals Are Stripping It Bare," *New York Times,* December 22, 1996, p. 3.

14. *RGC Forest Policy and Practice and the Case for Positive Conditionality* (London: Global Witness, May 1996), p. 4.

15. "Just Deserts for Cambodia: Deforestation and the Co–Prime Ministers' Legacy to the Country," (London: Global Witness, June 1997), p. 1.

16. World Bank, *1996 Cambodia Forest Policy Assessment* (Washington, DC: World Bank, 1996), pp. 39–41.

17. Gerry Hawkes, personal correspondence, January 10, 1997.

Building Democracy in Cambodia: Problems and Prospects

Lao Mong Hay

Introduction: Cambodia's Unstable Democracy

Democracy was born in Cambodia in 1947 when the country adopted its first constitution, which transformed the age-old absolute monarchy into a constitutional monarchy with multiparty democracy. Democracy started at a promising level in 1947 and remained there until 1955. In that year King Norodom Sihanouk, who had just succeeded in his crusade for Cambodia's independence from France, abdicated and formed a movement called Sangkum Reatr Nyum (People's Socialist Community), which, under the banner of "guided democracy," subsumed all political parties. The prospects for democracy began to decline when no other political parties were allowed to operate, press freedom was curbed, and genuine, competitive elections ceased to be held. Democratization continued to decline for a decade, as Sihanouk exercised autocratic power. The situation changed sharply in 1966, when Sihanouk no longer hand-picked parliamentary candidates, and all Cambodians were free to stand for the general elections. Power then shifted away from Sihanouk for several years, and hopes for a stable democracy remained high until Sihanouk succeeded in wresting back power.

In 1970 it appeared that Cambodia's democracy would reemerge when General Lon Nol toppled Sihanouk, and leading intellectuals seemed to have persuaded the new ruler to embrace multiparty democracy. But then Lon Nol became a dictator. In 1975 democracy's prospects bottomed out when the Khmer Rouge defeated the Lon Nol regime, assumed power, and brutally imposed their brand of radical agrarian communism. Hopes remained flattened following the ousting of the Khmer Rouge by the Vietnamese troops and during the People's Republic of Kampuchea (PRK) and the State of Cambodia (SOC).

Cambodian democracy began to revive in 1991, when the Paris Peace Accords gave it a new lease on life. In 1993 the Cambodian people bravely participated in free and fair elections organized by the United Nations Transitional Authority in Cambodia (UNTAC). The ascent of democracy was buttressed by the adoption of a new constitution that enshrined liberalism, pluralism, human rights, and the rule of law. Cambodian democratization remained at that level for a couple of years, then began to dip yet again when conflict intensified between the two major political parties, FUNCINPEC and the Cambodian People's Party (CPP). It fell almost flat, beginning on July 5, 1997, when Second Prime Minister Hun Sen used force to settle the contest and ousted the democratically elected first prime minister, Prince Norodom Ranariddh. Hun Sen has since become the de facto paramount leader of Cambodia.

This chapter examines the problems of and prospects for building democracy in Cambodia. It is written at a time at which democracy has been dealt a severe blow by the July 1997 coup. But it is also a time at which the prospects for national elections (scheduled for July 1998) hold the possibility, though not the promise, of a return to democratic politics and governance. The chapter takes a short- to medium-term perspective and suggests a number of ways the international community can help restore democracy in Cambodia.

The Immediate Challenge: Restoring Democracy Through Competitive Elections

Many Cambodians have been adversely affected by the events of July 1997. The direct victims include Cambodians who were killed or wounded, arrested or intimidated, or had their property stolen or damaged. Indirect victims have seen their livelihoods affected and now feel less secure because of the use of violence and the abuse of human rights. Factories and shops in the fighting areas were badly damaged. Thousands of jobs were lost overnight. Many foreign residents have left the country, and there are virtually no new investors coming in. Business enterprises have seen a decline in their activities, slowed their operations, and laid off employees. A wait-and-see attitude has prevailed in this climate of uncertainty. Tourists have not come; as a result, thousands of jobs in the tourist industry have disappeared.

Since the July coup the government and National Assembly no

longer reflect the will, wishes, and aspirations of the Cambodian people as expressed in the 1993 elections. The state organs are almost completely under the control of Hun Sen and the CPP, the losers in the last elections. FUNCINPEC, the winner of the 1993 elections, has disintegrated and some of its members have allied themselves with the CPP. Ung Huot, the unconstitutionally appointed first prime minister in replacement of Ranariddh, has no independence from Hun Sen. To many he is Hun Sen's puppet.

Despite the ouster of Prince Ranariddh and the evisceration of FUNCINPEC, Hun Sen and the CPP have not been completely successful in their grab for power. King Sihanouk has acceded to, but not approved, their takeover. Ranariddh and the other political leaders who fled Cambodia have mounted an international campaign to isolate the Hun Sen government. The international community has not condoned Hun Sen's use of violence to overturn the outcome of the 1993 elections. The Hun Sen government was unable to occupy Cambodia's seat at the UN. ASEAN has postponed Cambodia's admittance into the regional grouping until after the elections. The IMF and the World Bank have suspended their lending programs, and some countries have reduced or suspended their bilateral aid to Cambodia.

Diplomatic efforts have been made to ensure the safe return of the opposition politicians who fled the country in July as well as their freedom to carry out political activities. The UN has sent a small group of monitors to help in this effort. Sam Rainsy, the leader of the Khmer National Party, returned first and commenced straight-away to mobilize crowds to support him. An advance team of the Union of Cambodian Democrats (UCD), a loose coalition of opposition politicians who fled in July, returned to Cambodia in December 1997 to "test the waters." Prince Ranariddh returned in March 1998.

The focus now is on the upcoming elections. Before July 1997 these elections had been thought of as the way to resolve the escalating conflict between FUNCINPEC and the CPP; now they are seen as the means to restore democracy in Cambodia and as the solution to the present political and economic crisis. Preparations for them have been under way for over two years, and special efforts are being made to finalize them. The National Assembly has finally passed political party and electoral laws and a National Election Commission has been established. Technical and logistical preparations also are under way.

There have been positive developments with the return of opposition politicians and some degree of humility and flexibility on the part of Hun Sen after his government's failure to occupy Cambodia's seat at the UN. Hun Sen has yielded to pressure to strengthen the independence of the National Election Commission and to return to FUNCINPEC the control of its radio and TV stations seized during and after the July event. So far the returning opposition politicians have been safe and able to work without hindrance.

But a number of important issues remain unresolved. Fighting continues between forces loyal to Ranariddh and government troops loyal to Hun Sen. The Khmer Rouge continue their armed struggle and are reported to be allied with the Ranariddh forces. The CPP has virtually complete control over the state administrative apparatus and all security forces, which suggests that the elections will not be administered impartially and free of intimidation. The opposition parties do not have enough time to organize and prepare themselves for the elections. Doubts have been raised about whether Hun Sen and the CPP would be willing to relinquish power should they lose the elections—despite their reassurances of respect for the results.

The Long-Term Challenge: Building a Democratic Culture in Cambodia

The events of 1997 show that perhaps the greatest obstacle to democracy in Cambodia is the anti-democratic behavior of the nation's political elite. However, history, culture, and a low level of socioeconomic development are also obstacles—though not insurmountable—to building a democratic political culture.

Over the last century Cambodians have been ruled by a centralized and authoritarian French colonial administration, by an even more centralized and authoritarian communist system, and by a sometimes autocratic monarch. Until the end of the Second World War Cambodian rulers used the *chakrawatti* system to rule their country. This system was characterized by the concentration of power in the hands of one absolute ruler who tolerated no opinions different from his own. All viceroys and other officials had to submit unquestioningly to his rule and serve as his servants or instruments. These viceroys and other officials were, in turn, potentates in their respective domains. The Cambodian people were subjects of the king and serfs of the local potentates.

This dictatorial system could not fight off encroachments by Cambodia's neighbors or Western colonialists, and in 1863 Cambodia fell under French colonial rule. The French ruled Cambodia as despots; no Cambodians dared to challenge them. But the French did not remove or reduce the king's power over his subjects—even though in 1789 the French themselves had participated in an epoch-making revolution to overthrow royal absolutism. Thus Cambodia was under two layers of dictatorial rule: Cambodian royal absolutism overlaid with French colonial rule.

After the shock of World War II the French began to loosen their grip on their colonies, including Cambodia, by allowing them some degree of autonomy within the French Union. At the same time Cambodian elites who had been trained in France began to appreciate democratic ideas and some—in particular Prince Sisowath Youtevong—introduced them to Cambodian society when they returned home after their studies.

In 1946 King Sihanouk granted his people several democratic rights, including the right of association, the right of assembly, and the right to free speech. Political parties were formed, and elections were held for a constituent assembly. The Democratic Party headed by Prince Youtevong won and drafted the country's constitution. The 1947 constitution transformed the absolute monarchy into a constitutional monarchy and contained a chapter guaranteeing and protecting the fundamental rights of all Cambodians. Though still under French rule, Cambodia began to have liberal democracy.

However, soon after the county's independence from France in 1955, King Sihanouk began to curtail Cambodia's fledgling liberal democracy, and from 1955 to 1970 it was replaced by a guided democracy characterized by a one-party system of government. An attempt was made to restore liberal democracy in the early 1970s, but Cambodia's political leadership and government were so defective, and the strength of the Communist forces so overwhelming, that democracy was nipped in the bud. As a result a new layer of dictatorial rule, this time much more oppressive, brutal, and pervasive—that is, totalitarianism—took hold with all its savagery on Cambodia, claiming over a million lives and destroying or damaging all aspects of Cambodian society.

This history of autocracy explains—but does not justify—the rigid, uncompromising, and dictatorial attitude of many of the current political elite. While these leaders may have compassion (in the form of pity felt by a person in a superior position for a person in an inferior position) for the Cambodian people, they have little or no tolerance for any views or ideas that differ from their own or might challenge their position of authority. Given the absence of a tradition of tolerance, for the ruling elite the notion of "national reconciliation" means submission to their rule rather than compromise.

This problem with Cambodia's ruling elite is compounded by the fact that virtually an entire generation of Cambodians—those under the age of 35—has been deprived of an education and cut off from the outside world. And for the few who were able to attend school prior to 1993, their schooling was more indoctrination than education. As a result almost all of the nation's moral and ethical values have perished or been damaged. Now the focus of education, even at the primary school level, is on human resource development, which emphasizes developing Cambodians as economic resources rather than as thinking human beings and citizens. (There is a painful irony here in that under the Khmer Rouge, individually and collectively Cambodians became "labor units" to be used ruthlessly by those murderers.) Fortunately a small number of educated and skilled Cambodians survived the Khmer Rouge massacre, and many more have been trained since their downfall. But pervasive poverty, the persistence of traditional approaches to education, and the limited resources available for civic education have made it difficult to educate the majority of Cambodians about their rights and responsibilities as citizens. Until this happens the Cambodian elite will not be held accountable to the Cambodian people and democracy will remain vulnerable.

Finally it is often argued that the low level of Cambodia's socioeconomic development, particularly its low levels of income and literacy, make the country ill-suited for democracy. However, poverty is not an insurmountable hindrance to democracy in Cambodia, any more than it is in India or the Philippines. The main obstacle and danger to Cambodia's democracy is not the poor; rather it is the current ruling elite that undermines democracy and uses its wealth and power (and guns) to protect and enhance its position. This group is not keen to establish the system of checks and balances enshrined in the country's constitution. It breaks the law with impunity. One only need ask who in July 1997 resorted to the use of force to resolve a political conflict, causing the brutal deaths of over 40 Cambodians and severe damage to the livelihood of many others? It was not the Cambodian people who used force, violated others' human rights, and dispensed with democratic procedures.

Despite these obstacles and setbacks, there has been progress in building a democratic culture in Cambodia—especially when compared to the situation that existed before the UNTAC period. Not long after the adoption of the 1993 constitution, there were charges that democracy and human rights were Western values and could not fit in Cambodian culture. There were claims that democracy could only be achieved after economic development, raising the controversy whether efforts should be devoted to building democracy or economic development first. These two questions have now been largely resolved. It is acknowledged by most of the country's leaders that democratic values have Cambodian origins, in Buddhism, Cambodian literature, and even folk stories, and that democracy and development go hand in hand.

There is also a breakdown—though only partial to be sure—of the culture of silence inherited from the police states of the past. The print and electronic media have proliferated. Some newspapers are very critical of the government and its leaders. Cambodians can and do make representations on public issues (and personal problems) to government officials and members of parliament. Nongovernmental organizations have access to the state-owned radio and television stations to broadcast their educational programs, including debates on public issues. Some of these debates are critical of government policies. Finally there are also some signs of democratization at the local level. Democratic elections are being used to establish village development committees under the aegis of the Rural Development Ministry. And increasingly associations and nongovernmental organizations, including those at the grassroots level, are using democratic elections to choose officers and make decisions.

The Continuing Struggle to Enshrine Human Rights and the Rule of Law

Given Cambodia's history, it should not come as a surprise that reestablishing and strengthening the commitment of Cambodia's political leaders to human rights and the rule of law is a long-term struggle. Respect for human rights was officially stipulated in Cambodia's 1947 constitution, before the Universal Declaration of Human Rights of

1948. But over the last 50 years human rights in Cambodia have been routinely violated. During the Khmer Rouge era Cambodians inflicted upon their fellow countrymen some of the worst human rights abuses to have occurred during the twentieth century. The Vietnamese invasion and subsequent communist government ended the autogenocide, but human rights (as defined by the Universal Declaration) were viewed by the government as a hindrance to the country's much-needed national reconstruction at best and as a threat to the regime's power and the communist political system at worst.

The first substantial efforts to revive respect for human rights were made mainly by noncommunist anti-Vietnamese resistance forces. At a conference in Australia in January 1989 three of the four warring factions (except the Khmer Rouge) unofficially agreed to adopt the Universal Declaration of Human Rights. In the end human rights were accepted by all of the factions, and respect and observance of them were incorporated into the 1991 Paris Peace Accords.

Under the Paris Accords Cambodia was to respect human rights as enshrined in the Universal Declaration of Human Rights and other international instruments on human rights. The agreements state, inter alia, that "Cambodia's tragic recent history requires special measures to assure the protection of human rights and the nonreturn to the policies and practices of the recent past." An annex to the agreements fixed the principles to be included in Cambodia's constitution. According to the annex, the constitution will

> contain a declaration of fundamental rights, including the rights to life, personal liberty, security, freedom of movement, freedom of religion, assembly and association, including political parties and trade unions, due process and equality before the law, protection from arbitrary deprivation of property or deprivation of private property without just compensation, and freedom from racial, ethnic, religious, or sexual discrimination.... This declaration will be consistent with the provision of the Universal Declaration of Human Rights and other relevant international instruments. Aggrieved individuals will be entitled to have the courts adjudicate and enforce these rights.

The annex also stated that Cambodia will

follow a system of liberal democracy, on the basis of pluralism. It will provide for periodic and genuine elections. It will provide for the right to vote and to be elected by universal and equal suffrage. It will provide for voting by secret ballot, with a requirement that electoral procedures provide a full and fair opportunity to organize and participate in the electoral process.

All of these obligations were incorporated into the constitution adopted in September 1993. Like the 1947 constitution the 1993 constitution has an entire chapter devoted to human rights. But unlike the 1947 constitution the 1993 constitution recognizes that the disregard for human rights in Cambodia had resulted in the country's holocaust. Pluralistic liberal democracy is now enshrined in the constitution, and this provision on the political system cannot be amended.

Unfinished Institution Building

In Cambodia power tends to concentrate in the hands of one powerful man or a group of powerful men (politicians, generals, and businessmen). This concentration of power is an obstacle to the separation of powers and the workings of the system of checks and balances. Based on past experiences of Cambodia and a number of other developing countries, overreaching power is an enemy of political and economic development.

Cambodia's 1993 constitution mandates the establishment of a number of institutions, which, if they work properly, should provide ample checks and balances. These include the executive, the National Assembly, the judiciary, the Supreme Council of the Magistracy, the Constitutional Council, the king, and the National Congress. However, in practice there has not been an effective institutional separation of powers and to date the Supreme Council of Magistracy, the Constitutional Council and the National Congress are not operational or do not exist.

Many see the National Assembly, as it currently functions, as the rubber stamp for the executive. With very few exceptions members of parliament or the ruling parties have been coerced to toe the party line dictated by the party leaders. Very few have the courage to dissent. There is no order of importance and priority of laws in this new society in the making. Influential special-interest groups see laws that meet their demands enacted, while core laws to ensure law and order and regulate relations among citizens, such as criminal and civil laws, or laws determining the functioning of the constitutional institutions, have been relegated or neglected altogether. As a result there is almost complete anarchy in making and enforcing laws. The government and judges still apply old laws whether they are constitutional or not. As a result there are "a number of gaps, inconsistencies, and contradictions."[1]

King Sihanouk, as constitutional monarch, is expected to "reign but not rule." However, rather than being overly interventionist, as might have been expected, the aging and infirm king has been unwilling or unable to exercise many of his constitutional duties. For example, he has been unable to protect the rights and freedoms of his citizens or to ensure the independence of the judiciary, all of which are his constitutional responsibilities. More recently Hun Sen bypassed him altogether with the appointment of Ung Huot as first prime minister.

The delay in establishing the Constitutional Council and the Supreme Council of the Magistracy has undermined democracy and the rule of law in Cambodia. The Constitution delegates to the Constitutional Council the authority to interpret the Constitution, ensure the constitutionality of laws enacted by the National Assembly, and adjudicate electoral conflicts. Without the council there has been no mechanism for challenging the constitutionality of the actions of the Cambodian government or reviewing that of existing laws or new legislation. The Constitutional Council is supposed to be composed of nine members: three appointed by the king, three by the National Assembly, and three by the Supreme Council of the Magistracy.

The Supreme Council of the Magistracy is a judicial body responsible for ensuring the independence and quality of the judiciary. Chaired by the king, the Supreme Council has the authority to appoint and discipline judges. But more than a year after a law was passed establishing it, this body still has not been formed. In its absence there has been a lot of criticism of the judiciary, especially of the judges themselves, for their lack of expertise and impartiality. All of Cambodia's sitting judges have been appointed by the communist regime; only some have formal legal training, mostly in the communist legal system. Moreover the failure to constitute the Supreme

Council means that there are no members to serve on the Constitutional Council, as required by the constitution. With both Councils existing only on paper many seemingly unconstitutional laws and regulations remain in effect and few people have confidence in the independence of the judiciary.

Finally the National Congress is supposed to be a channel for the Cambodian people to voice their concerns over public issues and express their wishes and aspirations to public authorities, including their leaders. It could check the power of the government to some extent and make leaders more responsible to the public and accountable for their actions. But the political leadership has done little to establish the National Congress, and few Cambodians are aware that it is mandated by their constitution.

Political Parties and Democratic Competition

Another serious challenge to democracy in Cambodia has been the ongoing, recently bloody, contest for power between the CPP and FUNCINPEC, the two largest political groupings in Cambodia. Although nominally partners in the ruling coalition since 1993, these two political parties have continued to view politics as a "zero sum" game, wherein if one gains the other loses. Because of this they have remained fierce rivals, and each has sought advantage over the other rather than cooperation and compromise. Moreover both parties are highly personalized and factionalized, and few of the leaders of either have demonstrated a commitment to democratic decision making.

The rivalries between the two main parties have contributed directly to one of the major problems facing the nation: the bloated and corrupt government sector. Party-driven patronage and rivalry have contributed to the swelling of the bureaucracy to some 150,000 people and the maintenance of an army of more than 100,000 soldiers. (Programs intended to demobilize soldiers and reform the civil service, conceived at the beginning of the coalition government, have not been implemented.) This is far in excess of what is needed or can be financed. As a result civil servants and soldiers are paid subsurvival salaries, which leads to moonlighting, corruption, and worse still, extortion and other criminal activities. Equally important, moral and ethical values, a sense of duty, and loyalty to the government have largely disappeared from government service.

Still worse for the country has been the politicization and polarization of the civil service. Prior to the July coup most civil servants were loyal to their respective parties. Some superiors made decisions that served their party's rather than the national interest. Down the chain of command civil servants tended to obey and implement orders and decisions from superiors of the same party. This was prevalent from the national to the grassroots levels. Cambodia seemed to have three governments and administrations. Two were party governments, and the third was the Royal Government of Cambodia, in which both parties agreed on policies and implemented decisions together.

The 1998 elections are crucial to ensuring a multiparty system, a genuinely democratic National Assembly, and an effective government. Many Cambodians have enjoyed the new democratic system and want to continue along that road. While civil society groups are working to create a political climate and environment conducive to free and fair elections, the leaders and members of political parties need to do their part. Over the past five years politicians and political parties have laid bare their colors and spots. Some have lapsed into their old dictatorial ways, including the use of force, while others have been making efforts to prevent the return to serfdom.

With free and fair elections, the proportional representation system, and the participation of all opposition politicians, including Ranariddh, it will be very hard for a single party, however united and well endowed, to lawfully dominate Cambodian politics. The Constitution requires the support of two-thirds of those elected to parliament to form a government, and the quorum for meetings of the National Assembly is a high 70 percent of its members. As a result a party that may be dominant but short of the two-thirds in the National Assembly needs to mobilize the support of as many parties as possible to muster that requirement. A coalition may need to be hammered out, and even small parties with relatively few seats in the National Assembly may have bargaining power. However, the effective functioning of a coalition government and a multiparty parliament depends on the neutrality of the civil service and the security and military forces. It also depends on the independence of the judiciary, which can be brought about only by the activation of the Constitutional Council and the Supreme Council of the Magistracy. Democratic political competition will not survive for long in Cambodia if one side can use the power and resources of the state against its rivals.

The Role of Civil Society

Although still young and vulnerable, Cambodia's civil society—consisting of a variety of nongovernmental organizations, unions and professional associations, and the media—so far has shown some significant achievements. Cambodians, especially those at the grass roots, have appreciated the major contributions Cambodian and international nongovernmental organizations (NGOs) have made to socioeconomic reconstruction and development. Given the inability or failure of the government to provide basic social services, many Cambodians owe their survival or improved standard of living to these NGOs.

A number of Cambodian and international NGOs are also working to strengthen human rights and democracy in Cambodia. Many Cambodians were unaware of their human and political rights before 1992, when UNTAC started training and information programs to disseminate these values. Since 1993 Cambodian and international NGOs have built on these programs by carrying out activities designed to strengthen human rights, the rule of law, and democracy. They have included judicial, legal, and human rights training, disseminating information about human rights, the rule of law and democracy, and advocating and monitoring human rights.

Human rights training and information dissemination has been conducted through a variety of channels, including television and radio programs. It has been targeted at all sections of the population: the masses, civilian officials, the military and police, teachers and students, and even prisoners. As a result many Cambodians have come to know and understand the meaning of human rights and other democratic values and have asserted their rights through NGOs.

Throughout the country Cambodians are talking about the elections scheduled for 1998 and justifiably asking whether they can be held and be free and fair. Without some knowledge of democratic values, they would not be able to talk about elections in this way. Many of the NGOs concerned with human rights have joined forces in order to participate in the administration and monitoring of the 1998 elections. Two NGO coalitions have formed: the Coalition for

Free and Fair Elections (COFFEL) and the Committee for Free and Fair Elections (COMFREL). Both groups are cooperating in their efforts to provide voter education and poll monitoring. They are busy making preparations to provide such services to help ensure free and fair elections. But both need technical and financial assistance and support to do their work effectively.

Many Cambodian NGOs have continued to work hard to uphold the integrity of the pluralistic liberal democratic order that the international community helped establish in Cambodia—even in the difficult political environment following the July coup. With the suspension of some bilateral and multilateral economic assistance to the government following the coup, channeling humanitarian assistance to the Cambodian people through NGOs has proved an effective way to avoid punishing the poor. (These people and Cambodians in general are able to identify clearly who the international community "punished" for misconduct and deviation from that liberal order.) The role of civil society can be enhanced further by channeling more assistance to the Cambodian people through NGOs. These NGOs cannot undertake major economic and social infrastructure projects, but they are more effective and efficient than the bureaucratic machinery of the government, and they are capable of managing smaller projects that directly benefit the Cambodian people at the grassroots level. With more resources NGOs could undertake more projects to contribute to socioeconomic development and to the democratization process.

The Role of the International Community

The Cambodian people have benefited greatly from the sizable economic and technical assistance provided by the international community. Moreover the presence and support of international organizations, such as the UN Center for Human Rights and human rights and development NGOs, have helped to constrain the behavior of those in Cambodia inclined to disregard human and political rights. The actions taken by the international community during and immediately following the July coup—protection of threatened political figures, suspension of aid, and diplomatic interventions— helped to curb the violence and save lives. Without such prompt action the violence would have continued and there would have been more bloodshed and destruction.

The actions subsequently taken by some countries—the imposition of economic sanctions, the postponement of Cambodia's ASEAN membership, the decision to leave vacant Cambodia's seat at the UN, and continued diplomatic pressure—all have yielded positive results in the form of a degree of relaxation of control over the population, the openness to opposition politicians, and more liberal electoral and political party laws. These encouraging developments need to be nurtured and expanded upon in order to get Cambodia back on the track of full-fledged pluralistic liberal democracy.

The principle of noninterference in the internal affairs of sovereign states cannot and should not be applied strictly to Cambodia. Cambodia and the international community are bound together by the country's tragic history and the obligations inherent in the 1991 Paris Peace Accords and the 1993 UN-administered elections. Cambodia is at risk of slipping back to the autocracy and corruption that has characterized much of its past. The international community has both the right and the responsibility to keep this from happening. The international community can and should take action in the following areas to restore and strengthen democracy in Cambodia.

In the short run, ensure free and fair elections in 1998. The international community can and should play a major role in ensuring that the elections scheduled for 1998 are free and fair. To accomplish this the international community should take an active role, including using aid conditionality, as follows:

- Help create a less confrontational political environment by encouraging peace talks between the rival parties. Free and fair elections cannot be held in an environment characterized by violence and intimidation. The king should be encouraged to convene such a meeting between rival parties.
- Require and ensure that all opposition politicians, including Prince Ranariddh, are able to return to Cambodia to participate in the elections in safety, free of violence, intimidation, and discrimination. Require and ensure that all contesting political parties can campaign throughout the country free of obstacles and with equal access to the media.
- Require that the newly formed National Election Commission is independent, impartial, and has the financial autonomy and pow-

er to recruit electoral officers, determine its own rules and regulations, and give orders to all forces during the electoral period. The international community should set up a donor-steering committee to work alongside the National Election Commission to ensure the enforcement of electoral laws, rules, and regulations. This body should second at least two officials, a program officer and a finance officer, to the National Election Commission to help address technical problems and ensure the enforcement of a program of actions, rules and regulations, and sound financial management.

• Require that the government guarantee the rights, freedom, and security of domestic and international election monitors and provide financial support and technical assistance to domestic and international monitoring efforts. International monitors should be posted in all provinces and districts (around 200) to oversee the entire electoral process from the registration of voters to the taking of office by the winners. They should be assisted by local monitors provided by Cambodian NGOs. Donors also should appoint special monitors to ensure the enforcement of laws on the neutrality of the armed forces and of civil servants.

• In exchange for financial assistance require all competing parties to publicly pledge to respect the outcome of the election.

• Maintain the status quo with regard to Cambodia's ASEAN membership and Cambodia's seat at the UN until the elections are proven free and fair and the outcome is respected.

In the long run, assist the development of democracy. As the experience of 1993 shows, elections are a critical first step in the process of democratization, but elections by themselves do not ensure that democracy will take root. It is therefore essential that the international community look beyond the elections and continue to support Cambodian democracy in the following ways:

• Help to strengthen human rights in Cambodia by insisting on the trial of those responsible for the deaths caused by the March 30, 1997, grenade attack and the events during and after the July 5–6, 1997, coup. Those responsible could strike again and have an incentive to uphold the existing system that allows impunity.

• Help promote an independent judiciary and the rule of law by insisting upon the activation of the Supreme Council of the Magistracy and the Constitutional Council. Support the development of these bodies, an effective judicial system, and governmental and nongovernmental mechanisms to monitor and protect human rights.

- Encourage the Cambodian government to abolish the national army and simply maintain a professional police force to ensure law and order. The national army has a very dismal record. It has drained the country's meager resources, yet it has failed to defend the country or defeat the Khmer Rouge. Its soldiers and officers are among the worst violators of human rights. A Cambodia unarmed can protect itself better; a Cambodia armed is simply its own enemy. Improved relations with neighboring countries and the development of border regions are better defense of the country. The signatories to the Paris Peace Accords of 1991 should fulfill their obligations to guarantee Cambodia's territorial integrity.
- Help Cambodia to demobilize its soldiers and reduce the number of its civil servants. Help to find ways to increase the pay of those who remain and retrain them in order to have an honest, effective, and neutral civil service. Entrenched civil servants could be redeployed through decentralization and the creation of regional development boards, which would shift the focus of economic development from the capital and other major urban areas to the rural areas where the majority of Cambodians live.
- Support the development of civil society by channeling more assistance to NGOs in order to disperse powers from the center and away from one individual or group.

Conclusion

In the wake of the July 1997 coup the prospects for pluralistic liberal democracy in Cambodia look bleak. But one needs to bear in mind that Cambodia has tried a variety of regime types and political systems: Sihanouk's absolute monarchy, constitutional monarchy with multiparty democracy, Lon Nol's republic with dictatorship, and Pol Pot's and Heng Samrin's republic with communist dictatorship. Sihanouk's constitutional monarchy with multiparty democracy ensured peace, security, and some prosperity for Cambodians; all the republics with dictatorship led Cambodians to war and disaster.

Many Cambodians are speaking up against the deterioration of democracy in their country and are working to uphold the pluralistic liberal democratic order established by the 1991 Paris Peace Accords and the 1993 constitution. They are putting pressure on their leaders to honor what they had themselves agreed upon when they signed the Accords and adopted the country's constitution. They are mobilizing like-minded Cambodians to join in these efforts.

However, with leaders who are willing to use force and manipulation to stay in power, the intervention of the international community is still needed to convince Cambodia's leaders to respect the rule of law and embrace pluralistic liberal democracy. Absent sustained international assistance and pressure, it will be very difficult, and perhaps impossible, to return Cambodia's democratization to the upward path envisioned in the Paris Accords and desired by the majority of the Cambodian people.

Note

1. World Bank, *Cambodia: From Recovery to Sustained Development* (Washington, DC: World Bank, 1996), p. 23.

Cambodia and the International Community: The Road Ahead

Kao Kim Hourn

History

To appreciate the important role played by the international community in Cambodia today, one must first understand the country's tortured history. Upon gaining its independence from France in 1953 Cambodia began the process of nation building with sizable investments devoted to education, health, and infrastructural improvements. GDP began to grow and agricultural production increased during this period, making Cambodia one of the world's largest rice exporters. In 1967 Cambodia exported some 500,000 tons of rice, whereas in the immediate aftermath of the Pol Pot regime (1979) it was forced to import between 200,000–300,000 tons of rice. The international climate of the early 1970s, particularly the bombings of the country in Nixon's secret war during 1969–72 as a "sideshow" to the Vietnam conflict, led to the rapid reversal of these modest achievements and ultimately helped create one of the darkest periods in Cambodian history, commencing in 1975 when the Khmer Rouge came to power.[1]

The Khmer Rouge dismantled all existing state institutions and implemented a bizarrely misguided utopian experiment based on forced labor and total autarky, a brutal system without money, economic markets, private property, or human rights. An enormous loss of human capital followed. An extermination campaign was waged against the professional class, intellectuals, and skilled individuals, which drained Cambodia of its human resource capacity. This reign of terror lasted until 1979, but the misery and suffering as well as the

The author wishes to acknowledge the significant contributions of David J. Simpson in the writing of this article.

legacy of this vicious experiment continues.

In the aftermath of the Khmer Rouge's depredations and the 1978 Vietnamese invasion and occupation of Cambodia, the international community responded with an outpouring of humanitarian aid amounting to $700 million from 1979 to 1981, one of the largest international aid efforts of its kind. Most of this aid was channeled toward emergency refugee relief through multilateral organizations, such as the United Nations High Commission for Refugees, the International Red Cross, and other organizations assisting many refugees in Thailand and on the Thai-Cambodian border. Virtually no aid was dedicated to rebuilding Cambodia's shattered physical and human infrastructure.

International opposition to the Vietnamese-supported regime (initially the People's Republic of Kampuchea and later the State of Cambodia) resulted in the declaration of an economic embargo by most Western countries. The political dynamics of the cold war during this period meant that the plight of Cambodians was virtually forgotten. The Soviet Union and the Eastern Bloc states provided some support from 1982 until 1989; financial and technical assistance from socialist countries amounted to about $100 million per year.[2] But the rest of the world remained indifferent to the desperate needs of Cambodians during this period. As one observer noted, "even the UN turned a deaf ear."[3]

After years of indifference the international community, prompted by the withdrawal of the Vietnamese military from Cambodia and the vacuum left by the collapse of the Soviet Union in 1989, unleashed a barrage of nongovernmental organizations (NGOs) and bilateral aid to assist Cambodia in its reconstruction efforts. Cambodia was once again on the international agenda occupying a large space on the world stage. Interest in Cambodia was further stimulated by the Agreements on a Comprehensive Political Settlement of the Cambodian Conflict (Paris Accords) of 1991, which ultimately led to UN-supervised elections in May 1993. A total of $2 billion was allocated for the United Nations Transition Authority in Cambodia (UNTAC), which primarily supported peacekeeping operations prior to the elections. Bilateral and multilateral organizations promised an additional $2.3 billion in assistance for development from 1992 to 1995.[4] For a small country like

Cambodia, with a population of just 10 million, this international commitment can only be described as generous.

If the international commitment was great, so too were the problems. The challenges facing any new government of a "failed state" are difficult. These challenges were multiplied several times over in the Cambodian context of a depleted human capital, devastated physical infrastructure, underproductive agricultural sector, and fragmented political system. It was as if someone had picked up the whole of Cambodian society, shaken it violently, and then watched the pieces come down. This is the reality that faced the Royal Government of Cambodia when it took office in October 1993 after the adoption of the new constitution.

One of the first priorities was to jump start socioeconomic recovery and growth in Cambodia by simultaneously stimulating different economic sectors. The international community played a critical role in this initiative, providing assistance for basic infrastructure and training. It also provided breathing space for the government to enhance its political legitimacy by delivering basic goods and services to its citizens. The initial assistance was provided by bilateral and multilateral donors responding to the government's identified priorities. Most of the efforts toward the renewal and reconstruction of Cambodia were coordinated through the International Committee on the Reconstruction of Cambodia (ICORC). ICORC is made up of a variety of donor countries and international organizations. The principal donors are Japan, the United States, France, Sweden, and Australia. International organizations include the United Nations, the World Bank, and the International Monetary Fund (IMF).

The royal government also benefited from external assistance in the form of balance of payment supports from institutions such as the IMF through the Enhanced Structural Adjustment Facility (ESAF) and from the World Bank, plus some bilateral partners, in order to meet necessary budgetary requirements. In addition various bilateral and multilateral partners, including the Asian Development Bank, the UN Development Program, and a host of NGOs, also provided support for strengthening macroeconomic management and development. These efforts were significant to the achievement of relative economic stability in Cambodia during the 1994–96 period.

Today's Problems

Political stability has continued to be elusive. Cambodia's precarious political situation in the wake of the 1993 elections required that national reconciliation take a position of prime importance in the government's agenda. The coalition government attempted, with only modest success, to focus on political reconciliation and consensus building. The international community played an important role in supporting Cambodia's evolving democracy through awareness campaigns and diplomatic efforts and attempted, with mixed success, to serve as a watchdog over human rights. The events of July 1997 in which First Prime Minister Prince Norodom Ranariddh was removed from the leadership of FUNCINPEC has made this task more complicated, at least in the short term.

By 1996 a sentiment was emerging that Cambodia had already been given enough support by the international community, which would be well advised to scale down its financial involvement. Critics argued that other countries were more deserving and capable of using this aid more effectively. This sentiment has no doubt been given momentum by the unsettling events of July 1997. While one cannot deny that needs are great elsewhere in the world, a decision to "move on" would, at this point, be a grave error on the part of the international community. Such a decision would jeopardize the significant achievements accomplished over the last few years in Cambodia. Despite recent events Cambodia is on the road to progress and development, and it still needs support from the international community. The government seems willing to "take the training wheels off its bicycle" but it must have the reassurance that the international community will be nearby.

We live in a world of rapid technological change and split-second communications, but nation building does not occur overnight. It is a long, time-consuming process, particularly for a country with such a tragic past. Ultimately Cambodians are responsible for their own development and prosperity, but the international community also has an interest and a stake in seeing the nation succeed. As Cambodia is still among the poorest countries in the world, there is a certain degree of altruism in the international community that would tend to support its continued commitment. The international community has already made a significant investment in Cambodia; if it wants to protect this investment and ensure that

Cambodia does not slide back into chaos, it should continue to participate in the process of building a sound economy as the foundation of a stable society. The reemergence of crime and political instability in Cambodia would be especially costly for Thailand, Vietnam, and Malaysia and should compel them to take an active interest in their neighbor's progress. This will become even more relevant with Cambodia's eventual membership in ASEAN.

The ASEAN countries have made clear their desire for a secure and prosperous Cambodia as an important part of the plan to develop a united Southeast Asia. In particular, while nonintervention remains the cardinal principle for conduct among ASEAN states, the concept of "constructive engagement" is now being floated by such people as Malaysia's deputy prime minister Anwar Ibrahim, who had the following to say in 1996 at the Second International Forum on Toward One Southeast Asia in the 21st Century:

> [ASEAN] should not tolerate the existence of two regions, one prosperous and developed centered around the older members of ASEAN who had a head start, and the other poor and technologically handicapped, made up of the new ASEAN states. ... [ASEAN] cannot be oblivious to the problems of underdevelopment of the other members.[5]

Consequently we may see greater involvement in Cambodia by its regional cousins in part as a result of the July events. Thus far most of the involvement in Cambodia from ASEAN states has been in the area of foreign direct investment. Serious questions remain: What will be ASEAN's economic development obligations once Cambodia formally joins the regional organization? And to what extent should ASEAN assist in rebuilding the sense of political viability that was damaged by the July events?

The larger international community through the United Nations also has obligations to which it committed itself in the 1991 Paris Peace Accords. These include guarantees to assist and monitor the peace-building process, which is more than just the supervision of democratic elections. William Shawcross makes the case that the continued assistance of the international community is essential in ensuring social and political peace, which will then give rise to development and economic prosperity:

Determination by Cambodia's rulers will have to be matched by continued interest from the international community. There is a danger that the international attention that was so vital in helping Cambodia address its problems in recent years has now turned away in the belief that those problems are solved. They are not. Indeed, it should be clear from the Cambodian example that a peacekeeping mission needs follow-through and sustained commitment if, in the long run, it is to change a society. If the success of UNTAC is to be built upon, continued international interest, pressure, and assistance are vital.[6]

Successes and Failures

As with virtually every experience with international assistance in developing countries, there have been both successes and failures in Cambodia. The lesson learned from these experiences will help us better understand how future assistance from the international community can be improved. The term "international community" here refers to the United Nations and its various branches (e.g., UNDP, UNESCO, UNICEF, WHO, FAO, etc.), international organizations, and nongovernmental organizations, individually or collectively. International assistance has been effective in many ways in helping Cambodia emerge from a "failed state to a democratic one."[7] It has made contributions in the following areas:

Peace, Political Stability, and Security

Without considerable international assistance Cambodia could not have achieved even the very limited degree of political stability and security it has today. Building peace is a long-term process that requires much national and international effort in order to succeed. Fortunately for Cambodia, the international community has provided both moral and financial support. Its active interest will continue to be critical as Cambodia edges toward its second national elections in 1998.

Democracy

Given the recent political tensions and violence, the suggestion that Cambodia's democracy has been strengthened through the efforts of the international community may be shocking. However, Cambodia's democracy is only four years old and has made some clear advances during that time. Of particular note is the high level of consciousness among ordinary Cambodians of their democratic rights and liberties in the new society, even if there is little evidence of praxis. Democracy is not yet rooted in the country, but support from outside may be helpful in making it a reality. The role of the international community is not yet clear, but it is likely that foreign observers will help monitor the 1998 election, albeit with a smaller presence than in 1993. In the meantime the support for civil society through nongovernmental organizations continues through internationally supported training and awareness activities.

Stable Macroeconomics

As Cambodia moves from a centrally planned to a market-oriented economy, it is critical that it create a stable economic climate. International financial institutions such as the IMF and the World Bank have played an important role in supporting macroeconomic stability through various economic strategies and the implementation of structural adjustment policies. This type of support generates a favorable investment climate for investors, thus encouraging foreign investment and eventually enabling the private sector to become the engine of growth and development.

Land Mines

Cambodia is one of the most heavily mined countries in the world, and the international community has been very supportive in responding to Cambodia's needs with respect to training, research, mine removal, and advocacy. The international community's ability to mount an international advocacy campaign to ban land mines has been particularly noteworthy and would not have materialized without its input. This campaign may result in a universal ban on land mines.

Integration

International assistance has helped Cambodia to move toward regional and global integration. Cambodia was looking forward to becoming a full member of ASEAN in July 1997. Although admission has been delayed, Cambodia will eventually join. Successful and sustainable integration activities will involve high costs, increased human resource training, and greater exposure to the outside world after two decades of isolation.

While the benefits from aid have been notable, there are several areas where aid has failed or can be improved.

Dependency

To a degree, nongovernmental organizations, indeed the government itself, are still stuck in the emergency relief mode and have failed to make the transition to the idea of fostering development. Many organizations working in Cambodia since the crisis of the 1980s have not adequately addressed the shift in focus between relief and development. As a result dependency has been created among the beneficiaries. Cambodians have become familiar with the culture of international development and know what funders want to hear. They also have become too willing to allow different organizations do things for them. Cambodians must become more involved in their own development projects and take greater responsibility for their future. The issue of dependency is often difficult to address and must be dealt with on a case-by-case basis. However, in some circumstances the international community must be firm with the potential beneficiaries and ready to pull out of a project if an increase in dependency is seen. There are, of course, no scales to measure dependency, which makes the task of the international community even more difficult. However, as Cambodia matures the community should be aware of the potential hazards this may create.

Nonsustainable Projects

The goal of all development assistance should be to make the particular project sustainable after outside funding has ended. Unfortunately this is often not the case. One of the problems is the human resource deficit and lack of educated Cambodians, whose wages are high owing to the demand for skilled people. While international agencies often can afford to hire these individuals, local organizations find it difficult to employ them because of their high salaries. Another problem is the poaching of staff members. Unfortunately it is common for international organizations to hire Cambodians already working for another development organization by simply offering a higher wage. While the general motivation behind such moves is understandable, this practice should be discouraged; in countries like Cambodia with a limited pool of talent, no organization will be willing to invest in training its employees if all staff placements are subject to such poaching.

Project Survival

More thought has to be given to long-term project survival. Beneficiaries must be involved from the very beginning, and there should be a long-term plan that would allow the funding organization eventually to phase out its involvement. More organizations must be willing to hand over responsibility to local groups and people and allow them to make mistakes and learn.

Urban Bias

For various reasons, including security threats, the urban area of Phnom Penh has received a disproportionate amount of attention over the rural areas. This is a potentially damaging situation, especially as more than 80 percent of the population currently resides in rural areas. While Phnom Penh's economy is relatively well off, the rural areas are often neglected. The average monthly income is four times higher in Phnom Penh than in the provinces. Spending on education is twice as high in the city. What is perhaps more worrying is that the disparity between the urban and rural areas is increasing at an alarming rate. As one report states:

> Rural development is on everybody's lips in Cambodia and most actors recognize both the lack of rural development and the need for it. In spite of this, the pattern of heavy concentration of economic growth around the Phnom Penh area has not been broken. No matter how many studies point to the need for rural investment, this is, consciously or unconsciously, largely ignored by donors (whose agents mainly live in Phnom Penh).[8]

The same report revealed the concern of some officials within the Australian Foreign Ministry who worried that the economic unbalance may result in the repetition of the history of the 1970s. If development is to be sustainable it must address all parts of Cambodia, not just the areas most accessible to international officials, investors, and government officers. Some development organizations are doing a remarkable job in this area—but expanded efforts are necessary.

Communication and Coordination: Too Many Drivers

Communication and coordination among the various governments, international organizations, and smaller nongovernmental organizations can be improved substantially. Efforts are already under way to address some of these concerns and improve communication links and increase dialogue, and these must continue. At its annual meetings the ICORC had the potential to coordinate assistance among the international donors and the government, but this was never realized. Now as the ICORC is replaced by the World Bank–sponsored Consultative Group Meetings (CGM), it is hoped that aid coordination will be a higher priority.

Regardless of the outcome the international community must adopt an active communications policy both internally and externally, with a view to promoting mutual learning and cooperation. This also could include greater involvement in development policy debates at the national level and more structured links with other agencies and institutions. The royal government also has responsibilities to help coordinate international assistance by developing a clear set of priorities and needs. Naturally, it has taken time to elaborate the goals and prioritize the actions, resource requirements, and strategies initially presented in the National Program to Rehabilitate and Develop Cambodia. Nevertheless, the publication of Cambodia's First Socioeconomic Plan (FSEP) for 1996–2000 makes significant moves toward better defining the government's priorities.

In the absence of a clearly defined development policy and plan, projects and programs have evolved in an ad hoc manner. Consequently the opportunity to develop comprehensive and cogent approaches has been lost. This lack of a defined vision at the national level has led to the absence of a clear policy framework in several areas. The establishment of a coordination mechanism within the Council for Development of Cambodia (CDC) may be able to assure that Official Development Assistance (ODA) and investment flows are supportive of nationally determined priorities. The lack of coordination among donors has resulted in some duplicated poor aid management, particularly with respect to the technical assistance provision.

Thus far the government has welcomed development assistance from all categories of donor agency. This "open door" policy has meant that donors could operate in an environment where priorities have not always been clear and coordination of different activities to achieve common objectives has been less than successful. The almost total dependence on external funding for development expenditure has created a situation wherein international agencies working in Cambodia have often felt free to conduct themselves as they please with little or no coordination with the government or other agencies. Undoubtedly many of their initiatives may prove to be valuable, but even well-meaning assistance must respect the sovereignty of a democratically elected Cambodian government. Efforts to bypass the state only reinforce the weakness of the state and promote a lack of respect for the rule of law and the democratic process.

Some officials of international agencies often feel that they know better than the government or that they somehow have privileged access to the concerns of ordinary Cambodians. This may or may not be the case—the important thing is that information is shared among all parties and these programming decisions are made as inclusive as possible. The concept of sustainable development is in vogue with the international community at the moment, and it should therefore be well understood that along with environmental and economic sustainability the international community must also promote political sustainability. Once the international agencies have gone it will be Cambodians, both governmental and private, who are left to pick up the pieces.

Different Strokes

Finally, on the issue of aid coordination, different stakeholders have different motivations for providing assistance. Aid organizations often compete against each other in what has been termed "the dynamic of the aid market."[9] Often competition for aid contracts has meant that different organizations involved in development seek to establish their specialized niches, vigorously defending their area of specialization and sharing very little information with others. It is simple to predict that coordination will break down rapidly in such an environment. Various agencies have their own institutional survival to think about, which may force them to compete with other agencies. But some sort of conflict-resolution mechanism is needed to put the welfare of the Cambodian people ahead of these interinstitutional concerns.

Challenges Ahead

Cambodia has benefited immensely from the support of the international community as it travels down the road of development. The amount of assistance is significant, but then so was the crisis. Indeed the majority of funds have gone toward emergency relief and reconstruction rather than development per se. Similarly UNTAC's funds were directed primarily toward resettlement, repatriation, and peacekeeping.

An important shift in emphasis concerning external assistance took place in 1995 when international donors decided to pursue development instead of the previous reconstruction rehabilitation phase. The progression from emergency relief to development is an important one. It is not necessarily an easy transition because it involves a change in both outlook and philosophy. Unquestionably the emergency and rehabilitation efforts that were such an integral part of the initial international response were at least partially responsible for creating an environment of dependency among Cambodians. Nonetheless, it is important that we now move beyond this initial rehabilitation and reconstruction mentality to a more sustainable development approach. Both the Cambodian government and the international community must understand the significance of this shift in emphasis and come to realize the effect that this should have on their policies and programming.

Approximately 45 percent of the government's budget is derived from foreign aid. Most of this is directed to the public sector. While there is a plan to reduce the number of government employees, nobody quite knows how to achieve this, especially given the rather tense political situation. Such reform is vital if Cambodia is to develop a core group of qualified public sector employees for the effective governance of the country. Current public service employees are often poorly skilled, poorly paid, and therefore poorly motivated.

This desperate situation in public service has given rise to many dubious operational practices that are self-defeating in the long term. Moreover some of these practices seem to be encouraged by donors and condoned by the government. They include the provision of incentive payments to public sector employees to top-up their meager government salaries in exchange for being an "adviser" to a particular project. Although it may help the donor get things done, it does little to tackle public sector inefficiencies and has no sustainable impact except to skew salary structures.

Even if expenditures are controlled, the government will have to find an alternative revenue arrangement from the current one wherein 60–70 percent of tax revenue is derived from custom duties. As Cambodia prepares to enter ASEAN it will be forced to drop these tariffs and replace them with other means of raising revenue. Once again the emphasis must be on sustainable development; otherwise Cambodians are mortgaging the future of the younger generation.

"Sustainable development" does not only mean sustainable economic development but also sustainable political development. Cambodia is a particularly weak state and needs the international community to work with the government as partners, advisors, and friends. There is a tendency for the international community to focus primarily on economic stability with an assumption that as long as governments can deliver the goods (such as an annual 7 percent growth rate) they will enjoy political legitimacy. The Cambodian political situation is much too fragile to make this assumption. Domestic imperatives suggest that political stability is the key to development. Without peace and stability there can be no development. It is sad but undeniable that the events of July 1997 have complicated the achievement of internal stability, at least in the short term.

Sustainable political development can be supported from the international community through diplomacy and careful action encouraging democracy, human rights, and a free and independent judiciary in Cambodia. Local participation in decision making, especially in the rural areas feeling increasingly left out of the development process, must be encouraged. An excellent example of this is the UNDP's rural development initiative CARERE II, which uses a two-pronged approach that supports state capacity development while simultaneously promoting local participatory decision making. Currently there are no elected officials below the national level (commune elections have not yet been held) so there is little political legitimacy (democratic) at the provincial, district, commune, or village levels. The CARERE II program sets up a chain of elected committees from the village level on up. At the same time the project supplies the provinces with independent budget support from which they can fund "worthy projects" suggested by the villages and communes. This bottom-up approach empowers local community

members while building up the capacity of the provincial government and giving legitimacy to the formal organs of the state. While
mistakes will certainly be made, the project will be much more sustainable in the long term than a project implemented by an NGO
that undermines the authority of the state.[10]

While foreign involvement in the political sphere can be difficult in terms of respecting the legitimacy of a sovereign state, there
are still many areas in which they may participate, particularly in a
supportive role working with other Cambodians. An important area
that could be strengthened is the support foreigners could give to
local NGOs to grow and prosper. The capacity of local NGOs in
Cambodia must be strengthened—the creation of a meaningful civil society depends upon it. Once again this emphasizes the sustainable aspects of development, one that endures after the international
NGOs have gone home. It is not enough to simply employ
Cambodians in existing international NGOs (although this is useful). Endogenous development will occur only if local NGOs are
formed that are managed by Cambodians for Cambodians. The creation of a civil society in Cambodia depends upon it.

In terms of support for human rights outsiders must recognize
that the people of developing countries, their organizations, and
their governments play the central role and hold prime responsibility for achieving progress. The fundamental principles of human
rights are universal, but each society and each region crafts its own
approach, drawing on its culture, history, and political economic traditions. The international community plays a critical but supporting
role drawing on its own experiences. It should not attempt to export
particular institutions or practices but rather seek to work carefully
and sensitively with those in developing countries who are best
placed to achieve positive change. At times this may mean working
with the government rather than against it.

A question often raised in connection with international assistance is the issue of conditionality. Whether we Cambodians like it
or not, conditionality of aid or loans will always be used to pursue
the foreign policies of various countries or organizations in one form
or another. This is the prerogative of the donor country or organization involved. However, these donors must be realistic with their
demands and not impose conditionality in a reckless manner. This
involves identifying feasible options as well as outlining responsible

conditions for countries like Cambodia that must struggle daily with the realities of underdevelopment. The recent decision of the IMF to withdraw assistance from Cambodia because of the continuation of illegal logging in the provinces seemed a fair decision. However, the IMF should be clearer in its motives and avoid playing the role of environmental hero on this issue. The IMF does not so much care that logging continues in these areas; its concern is that revenues from these felled trees are poured into the National Treasury.

Conclusion

Cambodia has been the recipient of billions of dollars in assistance from the international community. While the amount of assistance may seem enormous to most international observers, most of the money spent over the years has been applied to emergency relief, not to development. While the process of rehabilitation, reconstruction, and development has been initiated, it will need to be sustained for at least a decade to come. Does the international community have the patience to endure another decade of international assistance to Cambodia? Some observers suggest that aid is an anomaly from a bygone era, while others have called for a rethinking of the entire concept. Most share the idea that current development cooperation must be reformed in order to ensure long-term goals. International development in Cambodia has matured to a degree that it is possible to discuss long-term goals with confidence. The task before us is therefore to commit to these long-term objectives in a cooperative and sustainable fashion so that Cambodia can rebuild itself and become a respectable member of the world community.

Notes

1. See William Shawcross, *Sideshow: Kissinger, Nixon, and the Destruction of Cambodia* (New York: Simon and Schuster, 1979).

2. John P. McAndrew, *Aid Infusions, Aid Illusions,* Working Paper No. 2 (Phnom Penh: Cambodian Development Resource Institute, January 1996).

3. François Ponchaud, *Cambodia: Year Zero,* trans. Nancy Amphoix (London: Allen Lane/Penguin Books, 1977), p. 215.

4. Actual disbursements of international aid during 1992–95 totaled only $1.3 billion—approximately $1 billion short of target. McAndrew, *Aid Infusions, Aid Illusions.*

5. Kao Kim Hourn, "Cambodia-ASEAN Partnership for Regional Peace," in *Peace and Cooperation: Alternative Paradigms,* ed. Kao Kim Hourn and D. Merican (Phnom Penh: Cambodian Institute for Cooperation and Peace, 1997), p. 169.

6. William Shawcross, *Cambodia's New Deal* (Washington, DC: Carnegie Endowment for International Peace, 1994), p. 1.

7. Statement by Madeleine Albright at 1993 Press Conference at Pochentong Airport, Phnom Penh.

8. Jan Ovesen et al., *When Every Household Is an Island: Social Organization and Power Structures in Rural Cambodia* (Phnom Penh: Swedish International Development Authority, 1995), p. 25.

9. B. Bernander et al., *Facing a Complex Emergency: An Evaluation of Swedish Support to Emergency Aid in Cambodia* (Stockholm: Swedish International Development Authority, 1995).

10. See Michael W. Doyle, *Peacebuilding in Cambodia,* IPA Policy Briefing Series (New York: International Peace Academy, 1996), p. 17.

Suggestions for Further
Reading

Contemporary Cambodia

Chanda, Nayan. *Brother Enemy: The War After the War* (New York: Harcourt Brace Jovanovich, 1986).

Chandler, David P. *The Tragedy of Cambodian History: Politics, War and Revolution Since 1945* (New Haven: Yale University Press, 1991).

———. *A History of Cambodia* (Boulder, Colo.: Westview Press, 1992).

———. *Brother Number One: A Political Biography of Pol Pot* (Boulder, Colo.: Westview Press, 1992).

Ebihara, May, Carol Mortland, and Judy Ledgerwood, eds. *Cambodian Culture Since 1975: Homeland and Exile* (Ithaca, N.Y.: Cornell University Press, 1994).

Heder, Steve and Judy Ledgerwood, eds. *Propaganda, Politics and Violence in Cambodia* (Armonk, N.Y.: M.E. Sharpe, 1996).

Jackson, Karl, ed. *Cambodia 1975–1978: Rendezvous with Death* (Princeton, N.J.: Princeton University Press, 1989).

Kiernan, Ben. *The Pol Pot Regime: Race, Power and Genocide in Cambodia Under the Khmer Rouge, 1975–79.* (New Haven, Conn.: Yale University Press, 1996).

Shawcross, William. *Sideshow: Kissinger, Nixon and the Destruction of Cambodia* (New York: Simon and Schuster, 1979).

The Role of the International Community

Brown, Frederick. *Cambodia and the Dilemma of U.S. Policy* <end> (New York: Council on Foreign Relations, 1991).

———. *Cambodia in Crisis: The 1993 Elections and the United Nations* (New York: The Asia Society, May 1993).

———, ed. *Rebuilding Cambodia: Human Resources, Human Rights and Law* (Washington, D.C.: Johns Hopkins University Foreign

Policy Institute, 1993).

Doyle, Michael. *UN Peacekeeping in Cambodia: UNTAC's Civil Mandate* (Boulder, Colo.: Lynne Rienner Publishers, 1995).

Findlay, Trevor. *Cambodia: The Legacy and Lessons of UNTAC* (New York: Oxford University Press, 1995).

Ratner, Steven and Jason Abrams. <ital> *Accountability for Human Rights Atrocities in International Law: Beyond the Nuremberg Legacy* (New York: Oxford University Press, 1997).

Shawcross, William. *Cambodia's New Deal* (Washington, D.C.: Carnegie Endowment for International Peace, 1994).

United Nations. *Agreements on a Comprehensive Political Settlement of the Cambodia Conflict* (New York: United Nations, 1992).

―――. *The United Nations in Cambodia, 1991–1995.* (New York: United Nations, 1995).

About the Contributors

David W. Ashley is a human rights monitor in Croatia for the Organization for Security and Cooperation in Europe. Prior to this he was UNDP/UNCHR advisor to the Commission on Human Rights and Reception of Complaints of the Cambodian National Assembly. He has been a researcher for Amnesty International on Vietnam/Myanmar. His publications include *Khmer Rouge Strategy Since UNTAC, Myanmar: "'No Place to Hide'": Killings, Abductions and Other Abuses Against Ethnic Karen Villagers and Refugees*, and *The Nature and Causes of Human Rights Abuse in Battambang Province*.

Frederick Z. Brown is Associate Director of Southeast Asia Studies at the Paul H. Nitze School of Advanced International Studies. His previous positions have been on the professional staff of the U.S. Senate Foreign Relations Committee and in the State Department Foreign Service. He has written extensively on Vietnam and Cambodia.

David P. Chandler is the author of six books on Cambodia including *Facing the Cambodian Past* (1996), *Brother Number One* (1992), and *The Tragedy of Cambodian History* (1991). As of fall 1998 he will be a visiting professor at the Paul H. Nitze School of Advanced International Studies. He has visited Cambodia numerous times since 1990 for his research as a consultant to Amnesty International, UNTAC, and the U.S. Department of Defense.

Michael W. Doyle is Professor of Politics and International Affairs, Princeton University, and Senior Fellow, International Peace Academy. He is the author of *UN Peacekeeping in Cambodia: UNTAC's Civil Mandate* and other works.

Kao Kim Hourn is the Executive Director for the Cambodian Institute for Cooperation and Peace (CICP) in Phnom Penh and an advisor to the Minister of Foreign Affairs and International Cooperation in charge of ASEAN Affairs. He is also a columnist for *The Cambodian Times*. Dr. Kao has authored numerous articles and papers on Cambodia, including "Peace and Cooperation: Alternative Paradigms," edited with Din Merican and published by CICP.

Lao Mong Hay is Executive Director of the Khmer Institute of Democracy in Phnom Penh. He was Acting Director of the Cambodian Mine Action Center from 1993 to 1994. From 1988 to 1992 he was concurrently Director of the Institute of Public Administration, Head of the Human Rights Unit of the Khmer People's National Liberation Front (KPNLF), and Aide to the KPNLF leadership.

Judy L. Ledgerwood is Assistant Professor of Anthropology at Northern Illinois University. Most recently, she was a Research Fellow at the East-West Center. In addition, she served as a Professor of Anthropology at the Royal University of Fine Arts, Faculty of Archaeology, Phnom Penh, Cambodia. She is the author of *Politics and Gender: Negotiating Changing Cambodian Ideas of the Proper Woman, Research, Education and Cultural Resource Management at Angkor Borei, Cambodia,* and other works.

Kirk Talbott is Senior Director for Asia-Pacific at Conservation International. Prior to this he was Director for Conservation Finance and Policy at the Nature Conservancy and the Asia-Pacific Regional Director for World Resources International. He is coauthor (with Owen Lynch) of *Balancing Acts: Community Based Forest Management and National Law in Asia and the Pacific.*

David G. Timberman is a consultant and writer specializing on Southeast Asian affairs and democratic development. Currently, he serves as a consultant to the Asia Society's Policy program and to the Asia program of the National Democratic Institute for International Affairs (NDI). He has held staff positions with the Asia Society, The Asia Foundation, and the National Endowment for Democracy. He is Director of the project on "Cambodia and the International Community."

Naranhkiri Tith has worked as a senior staff at the International Monetary Fund in charge of institutional building in economies in transition in Europe and Asia for 24 years. He has been an adjunct professor at SAIS since 1974, lecturing on economies of ASEAN and transition economies of the former Soviet Union and Eastern Europe. Dr. Tith also briefly served as Senior Advisor to the First Prime Minister of Cambodia and is founder of the Cambodian Development Council.